The Golden Step

A Walk through the Heart of Crete

by
Christopher Somerville

Armchair Traveller
at the bookHaus

Copyright © Christopher Somerville 2007, 2012

First published in Great Britain in 2007 by
Haus Publishing Ltd

This edition published in 2012 by
The Armchair Traveller
at the bookHaus
70 Cadogan Place
London SW1X 9AH
www.thearmchairtraveller.com

The moral right of the author has been asserted.

A CIP catalogue record for this book is available from the British Library

ISBN 978 1 907973 34 5
ebook ISBN 978 1 907973 33 8

Typeset in Garamond by MacGuru Ltd
info@macguru.org.uk

Printed and bound in the UK by CPI Group (UK) Ltd, Croydon, CR0 4YY

Contents

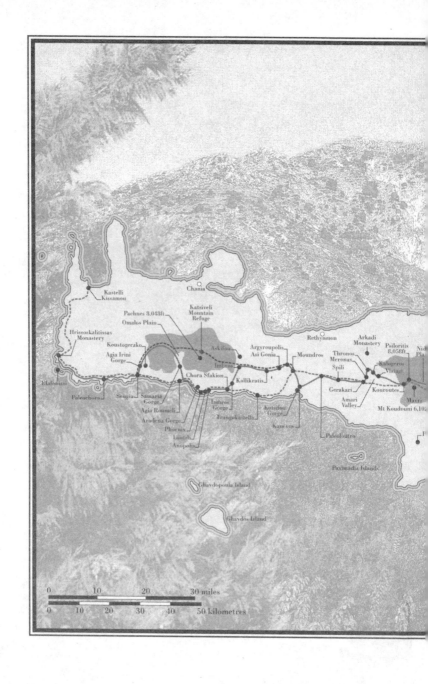

Kastelli
Kissamou

Chania

Pachnes 8,043ft
Omalos Plain

Katsiveli
Mountain
Refuge

Rethymnon

Arkadi
Monastery

Hrissoskalitissas
Monastery

Koustogerako

Agia Irini
Gorge

As-Kifou

Argyroupolis
Asi Gonia

Moundros

Psiloritis
8,058ft

Thronos
Meronas

Kalogeros
Vistagi

Spili

Imbros

Chora Sfakion

Kallikratis

Elafonissi

Paleochora

Sougia

Samaria
Gorge

Agia Roumeli

Aradena Gorge

Phoenix

Loutro

Anopolis

Imbros
Gorge

Frangokastello

Gerakari

Amari
Valley

Kourantes

Mt Koudouni 6,102

Kotsifou
Gorge

Kaneyes

Paleoloutres

Paximadia Islands

Ghavdopoula Island

Ghavdos Island

0   10   20   30 miles
0   10   20   30   40   50 kilometres

CRETE

Dia Island

IRAKLION   Knossos   Hersonissos
e of Winds   Phourni   Malia
     Archanes
akas 5,748ft   Mirtia
         Sgourokefali   Agios Nikolaos   Sitia
     Kastelli   Lato
     Kastamonitsa   Lasithi Plain
s Ilias   Angarathou   Psychro   Kritsa   Ano
tas 2,661ft   Monastery   Prina   Monastiraki Gorge   Papagianades   Zakros
          Mt Dhikti 7,047ft   Azari   Vori   Kato
          Katharo Plain   Vasiliki   Orino   Ziros   Zakros
                        Thripti   Chandras   Valley
             Ierapetra   of the
                   Mavros Kolimbos   Dead
        Mevdis Stavromenos 1,843ft

Chrisi Island

          ——————— Christopher's route
           - - - - - - - E4
           - - - - - - - E4 Alpine alternative
                    through White Mountains

For Jane, with love and thanks

Aphordakos

Aphordakos, great George: your hollow face
outcuts the wind, eagle nose discovers
lilies and painted saints. Between the squared
blocks of Minoan walls you find a place

for shards others would pocket. Aphordakos,
your mind hawks the hills, skims the rocks,
strung like a bow aimed for a shadowed peak.
Share your heights with me, great aegagros.

Talking to myself

In the bus to Sitia, staring out of the dusty windows at the lumpy land-scape of eastern Crete, I gave myself a proper talking-to. It was dog trouble once more, revisiting me like an ominous dream – bloody big shepherds' dogs, three of them, hunting me like wolves up a nameless dirt track. I had beaten off this evil trio many times in the week since my arrival in Crete, but still they rode my waking hours. Other apprehensions slipstreamed behind – staggering into a darkened village where every door was locked against me, tumbling headlong down the gorge side, lost on the mountain at nightfall. Yet at the same time raw excitement kept turning my heart over in my stomach.

Along with the diesel stink of the bus, this swerving between fear and elation, as if shuttling in an express lift, was making me feel physically sick. I unfolded my two maps of Crete, east and west, across the worn plush seat, and had a steadying look. Already their flimsy coloured paper, printed in Germany, was fraying at the seams. At a scale of 1:100,000 their uselessness to a walker intending to cross the mountainous island from end to end was only too evident. But in this year of 1999 they were the best on offer. They showed the bull-shaped island, familiar to me from many visits over the years, lying between the Cretan and the Libyan Seas. The stumpy hindquarters stretched east to terminate in the little cocked-up tail of the Sideros promontory. The blunt head with its three peninsulas – Akrotiri representing the rounded ear of the bull, Rhodopos and Gram-vousa the twin horns – pushed west. Actually Crete looked less like a bull than a rather scrawny and etiolated rhinoceros. Dotted along its north coast at regular intervals were the chief towns of the island – Chania and Rethymnon the elegant Venetian queens of the west, Iraklion (where I had boarded this bus a couple of hours ago) the dusty and noisy capital city in the centre. A little further east lay Hersonissos and Agios Nikolaos, the play-towns of, respectively, more and less downmarket tourism. Out towards the far east the map showed the compact regional centre of Sitia, where the bus driver would be putting me down in an hour or two.

Two other places stood out. I had ringed them round in black ink. Below the Sideros promontory, tucked into a bay at the easternmost end of the island, was the seaside hamlet of Kato Zakros. By the road into the village the cartographer had placed a symbol, a little red classical column. 'Antique Place,' said the key. The 4,000-year-old palace of Zakros lay here, one of the greatest treasures of Crete's Golden Age of Minoan civilisation. At the western tip of the island, about 200 miles away as the crow flew, sat a tiny black square topped by a cross. 'Moni Hrissoskalitissas' was printed alongside in scarlet – the Monastery of the Golden Step. Legend said that one step in the flight of 62 that leads up to the monastery was made of gold; but only the pure in heart could see it.

I stared along the map, holding it still against the jolting of the bus. Between the eastern and western extremities of Crete lay four ragged areas where the gentle green of lowland country changed colour to a drab olive brown and the contours ran together in bunches. These were the four mountain ranges that made up the lumpy spine of the bull island – Thripti, Dhikti, Psiloritis and Lefka Ori. The latter and more westerly pair were generously overspread with paler patches where the land rose over 7,000 feet above sea level. From previous climbs and dirt road drives I had gathered a very rough impression of these mountains – their fierce gorges, their spiny vegetation and rubbly limestone paths, their overhung cliffs and great scrubby slopes falling into shadows; above all, their lonely stretches of mile after rocky mile with no other human in sight. The map breezily ignored these realities. It showed a footpath running from east to west across the whole island, a red wriggling line about 300 miles long, labelled 'European Hiking Route E4', marching confidently all the way from Kato Zakros to Hrissoskalitissas with never a doubt in its head, hurdling mountains and striding across lowlands with equal nonchalance. Just follow me, it seemed to say. Bob's your uncle. What's the problem?

No problem – except that I had been doing a little checking up online and among personal contacts, and was pretty clear that European Hiking Route E4 was in truth a poorly way-marked, barely visible apology for a path, a fickle companion liable to sneak away and hide when the going got rough in the wild uplands of Crete. It was up in such high and lonely places that my overactive imagination had set all those troubling scenarios of dog attacks and inaccessible crags I had improbably scrambled to. Yet paradoxically it was the mountainous interior of Crete that had called to me from the very first day I had set foot in the island many years before.

The coasts of Crete are famous for their beauty. Each sandy bay looks as if it has been arranged by an exterior designer for the exclusive appreciation of discerning persons. The seas are warm and of an irresistible inshore turquoise that shades out into inky blue. Mountains slope seductively to cliffs and coves. The bathing, sun-worshipping, beer-sipping life never seems more seductive than in the coastal havens of Sougia, of Xerokambos, of Falassarna and Tholos. But my Cretan eyes, somehow, were always lifted to the hills. This must have been largely thanks to George Psychoundakis and his wonderful book *The Cretan Runner*. I'd first devoured this classic account of the Second World War resistance in German-occupied Crete as a teenager, reading my father's battered old copy. Psychoundakis was a shepherd boy from Asi Gonia in the eastern skirts of Lefka Ori, otherwise known as the White Mountains. In his late teens in 1941 when the Germans invaded and took over his native island, he joined the *andartes* or resistance fighters as a runner and carrier of messages. He ran, climbed and walked all over Crete in his cracked shoes. The book he wrote about his experiences among those incredibly brave and hardy men and women of the Cretan Resistance, translated after the war by his field commander Patrick Leigh Fermor, filled me with passion

3

for the mountains of Crete and gave me a goal – to walk one day in the footsteps of George Psychoundakis.

I loved wandering the high back country of the island, stumbling on village dances and church feasts, watching people take the kind of time and care in the steep mountain fruit and vegetable gardens that most coastal places with their tourist money seemed to have turned their backs on. In the upland villages of Kritsa and Thronos I made local friends who took me hiking among the hard clinkery hills, orange and white limestone wildernesses splashed with a brilliant palette of small flowers, sun-baked villages on dirt roads that snaked among olive and citrus groves. One evening in the Taverna Aravanes at Thronos when friends were singing *mantinades*, pungent little verses that fly back and forth across the table to tease, provoke and point up the singer's cleverness, someone – it was a stranger, and I never found out anything else about him – produced a phrase as he tried to translate one of the mantinades into English for my benefit. 'They are singing,' he said, 'that Crete is a place of earth, and it is also a place of dreams.' I never heard that mantinade again, but the phrase stuck fast in my mind as entirely apt, complete in itself. I told myself that I'd learn more and better Greek than my few rudimentary 'yes-no-please-thanks-hello-goodbye' phrases, and I'd set out one day to explore the island of earth and dreams on foot in one continuous end-to-end burst, with a walking stick in my hand.

A nice romantic pipe-dream, not to be taken seriously for a moment. And there it would probably have rested, if it hadn't been for the advent of my 50th birthday and the present that my wife had secretly decided to give me. It was a wise gift, a loving and a generous one. 'I don't want to give you any *thing*,' Jane said. 'What I want is to give you a stretch of free time. Two months, say. I'll hold the fort at home, I'll look after the children and pay the bills and all that stuff. Just go and do something wonderful, something you've really longed to do. Something for yourself.'

Middle-aged men in the midst of their working lives don't get offers like this. We push our ostrich heads down the burrow labelled 'too busy to live', and the other one signed 'time running out', and there we stay, pinned

4

to the ground by our own lethargy and fears and nice comforting tunnel vision. Now I was to be jerked out into the open – a scary prospect. What on earth should I do with this unlooked-for slice of freedom? Something that would take about two months; something entirely selfish, something for myself. There was only one answer, really. I'd do the Cretan mountain walk. And I'd do it as much in the spirit of George Psychoundakis as I could, with as little technology as possible. I didn't want buttons and switches and batteries to get between me and the raw experience, and anyway machines always fell to pieces if I tried to employ them. I wouldn't take a Global Positioning System device – partly because I'd have to learn how to use the wretched thing, but mostly through sheer bloody-mindedness. Map and compass would do. No mobile phone to help me if I got into difficulties; I'd rely on any common sense I might discover in my possession, and on any Greek I could manage to scrape up along the way. No collapsible walking poles or high-tech trainers or other fancy-dan apparel to distance me yet further from the shepherds and farm women and village children I'd be talking to. I'd wear ordinary boots and clothes and I'd carry the *katsouna*, the white figwood walking stick, that I'd been given by friends in Kritsa. Just how much of an ice-breaker that katsouna was to prove, I did not then imagine.

The one electronic device I would allow myself, thanks to a well-honed apprehension about stray dogs (I had encountered on past occasions the immense wolf-like beasts the Cretan shepherds called dogs, far from their masters and keen to show me all their teeth), was a Dog Dazer, a clever little gizmo that emits an ultrasonic scream, inaudible to humans but highly unpleasing to dogs. It had saved my ankles several times before, and also provided a moment of high comedy on a previous occasion when, walking with a party of Americans in the hills of Provence, a pair of local Cerberuses had come racing at us out of a farm track. When I pressed the Dazer's button the dogs screeched to a halt cartoon-style, did a music hall double take, and ran off yowling into a cornfield. 'What happened to them?' my companions wanted to know. 'Oh, it's a kind of high frequency ray that jellies their brains,' I deadpanned, trying to be funny. 'I killed 'em.'

Never in the field of human irony-bypass can eyes and mouths have opened so wide. 'Oh – my – *Gaahd!*' they gasped. 'You … you *killed* them? Oh, the poor, poor things! Quick, we must find their owner and … Oh my God, what if he sues? Who's got any cash?' The whip-round was well under way, and the Somerville name turning to the muddiest shade of mud, by the time I managed to demonstrate the Dazer's harmlessness on a nearby cow. But I don't think the Americans ever quite believed anything I told them after that. I kept catching them looking sideways at me.

'Go where you want and do what you like,' Jane had said. 'There's just one prohibition. No writing.' That was a shrewd blow. I had been making a full-time living as a travel writer for the previous ten years. Travel writing is a precarious business, very much subject to the whims of fashion and the caprices of commissioning editors. He who keeps a full wall planner survives. Every trip taken, every family holiday, every walk in the country becomes a means of generating income. A Sunday afternoon stroll with friends in the Cotswolds? Turn that into a Walk of the Month for the *Daily Blah*. A family week in Cornwall? 'How to Amuse Stroppy Teen-agers on Holiday' for the *Sunday Sloth*. A sudden summons to London? 'Ten Museums in Half a Day' for *Jabberwocky Magazine*. And so on. Without my wife's embargo I'd be scurrying round for Cretan commissions; I'd take every sidestep to every famous site; I'd arrange 'just an hour, honestly' meetings with tourist representatives. I'd be note-taking all day and scribbling all night. There would be pressure to perform, to move along, to get somewhere and do something. In other words, I'd be tense all the time and I wouldn't see a thing.

Drop all that, was Jane's injunction. Go with the flow. If you want to stop, stop. If you want to walk on, keep going. If someone invites you, say yes. If you can't be arsed to visit this or that site, then don't. You're not writing a guidebook, or any sort of book. You've been living by timetables and in the future far too much. Don't plan this adventure; let it happen to you, day by day. Live in the moment, just for once. If you're going to have this experience, then for heaven's sake have it to the hilt and beyond. Otherwise, do something else.

That was fantastically liberating, and also quite frightening. How was I actually going to cope with two months of not working, of not worrying about anything except how to get from A to B over tough terrain, and how to secure a plate of food and a bed for the night when I got there? How could I prevent myself transferring my time-of-life anxieties to the trip, to the route, to my welfare, to a hundred and one potential bugbears? There and then I made a resolution to try to trust to common sense and the kindness of strangers. The latter I knew I could rely on – Cretans, especially mountain dwellers, are some of the most hospitable people on earth. The former I was more dubious about.

The fact is that travel writers, in their operations for national newspapers and magazines, have a very unreal experience of travel. Someone offers, arranges and pays for your flight, your hire car and hotel. A charming sticky-haired girl in a red bolero meets you at the airport with a sheaf of booklets and maps, with complimentary passes and a timetable which, if you don't hold out against it, will skewer you to five dawn calls, five long lunches, five very long and boozy dinners, ten coffee meetings ('including the Mayor of the Regional Commune and the Head of the Bureau of Local Initiatives Touristical'), and twenty trips with a driver and interpreter whose English is just a little better than yours to visit a brand new tourist attraction that will make you an hour late for your next coffee meeting with the promoter of a rival attraction forty miles down the highway. Unless you are very firm about being left to your own devices and finding your own story in your own way, you can wake up one day to find that your powers of planning and thinking and acting for yourself have leached away. You can actually discover that you are *frightened* of travel, in the sense that proper travellers of the calibre of Freya Stark or Wilfred Thesiger or Patrick Leigh Fermor would have understood it: a setting off into the unknown and unpredictable. And you can certainly find that those powers you once took for granted as innate – knowing intuitively the direction to head for, finding the right place to doss down under the stars, making the best of a bad job in adversity, lucking across the very person who can help you out of a fix – have become blunt and unreliable. I wasn't sure just how much I had declined towards becoming a tourist rather than a traveller, and this was the perfect way to find out.

I petitioned for, and was granted, permission to keep a journal of my wanderings. Other than that, it would be Jane's way for me. And as soon as I decided to let it all just happen, things became a whole lot easier. I fixed up a few lessons in Greek with Aglaia Hill, a charming Greek-born teacher who lived a few streets away from me. We had great fun devising a personalised phonetic phrase-book, all the way from *Meé-pos échete thomátio ya ména?* ('Do you by any chance have a room for me?') to *Oníra gliká!* ('Sweet dreams!') and my favourite, a fiercely shouted *Páre ta skiliá!* ('Call off your dogs!'). Preparing for the walk now was merely a question of deciding how little I could get away with carrying on my back, filling my pockets to bursting with drachmas, and fixing a date. Greek Orthodox Easter seemed a good and suitable time to start the walk in Kato Zakros. Springtime in Crete should guarantee decent weather (I could take a risk and leave the tent at home), and there would be sheets of wild flowers all the way. I could hope to reach Hrissoskalitissas monastery just in time for Whitsun, which would nicely book-end the adventure. And a Cretan Easter with its processions of flowers and candles, its midnight feasts and shattering volleys of firecrackers would be a great send-off, too.

〜

Arriving in Iraklion with a few days to spare before the Easter celebrations, I made straight for the premises of SOHI, the Iraklion branch of the Greek Alpine Club. It was the Greek Alpine Club that had initially surveyed and way-marked European Hiking Route E4. A phone call to its secretary Kitsa had convinced me that among the members of the Club lay my only hope of finding someone to tell me at least something definite about the mountain path, already assuming a mythic or dream-like quality in my inner eye thanks to a complete absence of hard information on its terrain, its present state or even its actual whereabouts. 'You'll find us up the stairs at 53, Dikeosinis Street – but only between 8.30 and 10.30 on weekday evenings,' Kitsa warned me over the phone. 'We Cretans are proper mountaineers, you know, and during daylight ... well, we like to be up in the mountains.'

Seeds of my Cretan odyssey had been sown several years before by Charis Kakoulakis, erstwhile President of OYK, the Long Distance Club of Crete. Charis is a wide-screen dreamer, fingerer of many pies and passionate man of Crete. He had been my friend, educator and Mr Fixit in Crete for ages. His work as press officer for the island's tourist organisation, fantastically haphazard in most respects, was the anchor that prevented Charis from floating clean away on a sea of wonderful schemes. But the great Minoa Kelefthos trans-Cretan running race was his very special baby from the start. 'Christopher,' he'd rhapsodised in his airless Iraklion office, 'this is going to be a very bloody marvellous thing. Everyone will come to Crete and we will give them all hospitalities. Everything will be very nice,' and he emphasised the point with a patent Charis gesture, forming a circle of completion with forefinger and thumb, then making a horizontal pass with it in the air that drew a definitive line under an invisible apex of perfection.

A noble idea that briefly found its moment in the early 1990s, the Minoa Kelefthos super-marathon invited the world's elite long-distance runners to compete in the most gruelling of mountain races from end to end of Crete. Their course, the reverse of mine, started with morning prayers at Hrissoskalitissas monastery out west, and finished twelve days and some 300 miles later with a sizzle of tortured feet in the sea at Kato Zakros in the east. On the steepest stages – the inhospitable White Mountains of the west, the ascent of the fearsome 6,000-ft deep Samaria Gorge, the slopes of Crete's highest mountain, Psiloritis – participants were permitted to slow to a walk. Elsewhere it was all running. The terrain was consistently rubbly and breakneck, ankles always likely to be turned or broken. Vertical drops and fathomless sinkholes were often only a stumble away. Rest stages – typically a mat on the floor of a village hall – were few and far between. All the competitors gained at the end was honour, glory and a pair of battered feet.

Remarkably, no-one died or was seriously hurt. Even more astonishingly, some of the pioneers and a handful of acolytes came back for more punishment over the same course a couple of years later. The whole splendid enterprise fell apart after that, a victim of lack of money and leadership. But the Minoa Kelefthos had left an intriguing legacy – the idea that the whole length of Crete could be travelled on one continuous footpath, and not necessarily at the double. Where runners had blazed the trail over mountains and down screes, through forest and up gorges, walkers might follow. I was powerfully drawn to the notion, and even more so when I discovered on looking more closely at the maps that the Minoa Kelefthos runners had in fact been mostly following a route that had already been surveyed, brought into being and waymarked as European Hiking Route E4.

The European Hiking Routes, numbered 1 to 11, were the brainchildren of the European Ramblers' Association, founded in Germany in 1969. It was another noble idea: Europe's citizens in free flow across cultural and political borders, carrying with them the healthful spirit of internationalism as they strode from Sweden to Italy along E1's string of high paths, or followed E3 from Santiago de Compostela on the stormy Atlantic coast to the shores of the Black Sea, or ventured the 3,230 miles from Lapland to the Aegean Sea along E6's mighty southward course. The notion of Spaniard and Bulgarian meeting with broad smiles and hearty handshakes among the Carpathian mountains of the Czech Republic, or Finn and Greek slapping each other on the back in the Austrian Alps, is a great and inspiring one. The fact that, in a purely practical sense, no rambler would be likely to find the time, the money or the multiple languages to accomplish the European Hiking Routes is by the way. More to the point, standards of way-marking and of maintenance of the E-paths by volunteers have varied enormously from one country to the next. Those European nations with a deep-rooted history of long-distance leisure hiking, such as Germany and Austria, tend to keep their European Paths in good order. Those without such traditions are less enthusiastic, more neglectful and more strapped for cash, a manifestation that becomes more marked the further south one looks. Crete, as a glance at the map shows, is the most southerly place in Europe.

Kitsa turned out to be a bird-like woman in her early 60s with a pair of very sharp eyes. With her in the little club room at the top of the stairs sat two younger men. Pantelis Kampaxis was a slim, athletic chap of twenty-something, with plenty of charm and a nice girl by his side. The other man – 'Pantatosakis, Iannis,' he introduced himself formally, adding a bone-crusher handshake – a former hero of the Minoa Kelefthos race, looked most impressive, a low-slung and stocky Hercules with a black beard and close-cut hair flecked with silver. Together we spread out my two pathetic-looking maps with their unconvincing red threadworm of a path. Iannis Pantatosakis stabbed his strong forefinger at various points along the route and shot out terse descriptions of each successive section, while I scribbled frantically in my notebook. The phrases fell like tablets of stone from the mountain: 'Good road ... asphalt from here to here ... good road ... dirt road ... water here ... shelter there ... little bit problem here ... dirt road ... good road ...' From what I could gather during this two-minute seminar, the whole trip would be a breeze, a gentle wander all the way on asphalt or dirt roads. Looking furtively at the mighty calves and barrel chest of Pantatosakis, his air of frighteningly hardy self-reliance, I wasn't entirely convinced by the dismissive 'No problem, it's very easy' with which he concluded his survey.

Soon Pantatosakis, a man clearly ill at ease between four walls, was on his way down the stairs, three at a time. When he had gone, Kitsa and Pantelis Kampaxis filled me in on a few realities. I couldn't quite make out how much of the route was actually visible as a path on the ground, but it was clear that the Cretan leg of E4 was in an unfinished state. The route was supposed to be way-marked with 'E4' signs in yellow and black, mounted as tin cut-outs on tall poles or painted onto prominent rocks along the way. But rain, sun, snow and itchy goats in search of a scratch-ing place had worn away many of the painted signs, while most of the pole-mounted markers had been taken for souvenirs, snapped off for vandalistic fun, or shot full of holes by shepherds at target practice. One particular section, the seemingly straightforward run of coast between Agia Roumeli and Sougia towards the end of the walk, they wouldn't recommend I touch with a barge-pole. 'Very bad marking,' said Kitsa, frowning, 'very bad path – many cliffs. It's easy to lose your way, and if you break your leg you can lie many days with no help.' There seemed to be little formal accommodation along the route in terms of hotels or bed-and-breakfast places, though Kitsa and Pantelis both thought that hospitality towards the stranger still held good as a rule in the small hill villages and the scattered shepherds' huts in the mountains. And there were a couple of sections where I was definitely going to need some help with wayfinding for a day or so – making my way across the tangled landscape of the Dhikti Mountains south-east of Iraklion, climbing a still snow-clad Mount Psiloritis in the centre of the island, and crossing the high inner fastnesses of the White Mountains in the west, where sudden fogs could descend at this time of year and late-lying snow bridges hid sink holes many hundreds of feet deep.

'Would anyone be free to walk those parts with me?' I asked. Tough young Pantelis looked me over consideringly, plainly wondering if I was up to it. 'I can come with you, depending on the weather,' was his verdict. I walked back to my hotel delighted at the prospect of his company, but more apprehensive than ever about what I was letting myself in for.

Swallows newly arrived from Africa were skimming across Platia Eleftherias, brushing through the trees with soft explosive sounds, and I thought of them winging onward to England. Another harbinger of spring, Charis Kakoulakis, eventually turned up at the hotel, late as usual, rushed as usual, as full as ever of enthusiasm, helpful advice and optimistic purpose. Flecks of lemon blossom still clung to his hair from an afternoon feast on some terrace somewhere. The tickle of his large moustache in my ear was a well-remembered keynote of his embrace. 'I am one hundred percent sure that you will have no problem about finding the way or where to sleep. Just ask for the village priest or school teacher, and everything will be well.' He drew his characteristic line through the air with O-shaped thumb and index finger to indicate something inexpressibly complete and good. 'In Ziros ring this friend of mine, Mr Kharkiolakis – he'll give you a room. In Papagianades you will sleep at the school for police officers – ask for *skolí tis astinomías*. Orino, that's a rich village, three tavernas, you will have no problem. At Kritsa you will ask at the *kafenion* of the Aphordakos family ...' and so on and on, all the way across my maps, abolishing distance, time and difficulties with equal insouciance. It gave me confidence – greatly exaggerated, as things turned out, but a welcome boost at a time of low ebb.

⁓

Now here I was in the bucketing old bus, grinding slowly east from Iraklion, feeling queasy, trying to ignore yet another attack of cold feet. It was a relief when we finally got to Sitia and I disembarked to find the whole town revved up for the holiday. No time for thinking or worrying now; best just to take a deep breath and plunge in.

All Good Friday the amplified voices of priest and cantors, tremendously tinny and lugubrious, poured forth into every crevice of the town. In the late evening I followed the crowds up the hill to the Church of Ayia Aikaterini. The interior was a blaze of candlelight, out of which the deep, doleful chanting of the priests floated to mingle with the funereal donging of the church bell. Young girls and old men went along the line of icons in the porch, reverently touching their lips to each one.

Soon a squad of boys in blue uniforms and berets appeared in the doorway, carrying the *epitaphios* – a model bier shaped like a miniature domed church, covered in a thick mantle of white flowers. They swayed it along the streets in procession, convoyed by lanterns on poles and a candle-bedecked cross, a brass band adding a background thump and blare. I joined the flow of the crowd that shuffled slowly after the funeral party, many thousands strong, a thin brown candle flickering in every hand. Answering twinkles came from the balconies of apartments along the road, where families leaned over to sprinkle us with rose-scented water or waft incense smoke across our heads from tiny brass braziers. The caged finches and linnets that spend all day singing their little jailbird hearts out so poignantly on the balconies had woken up, confused by the lights and noise, and the sweet trickling notes of their false dawn chorus rose momentarily here and there before sinking back under the bumpity-bump of the marching band.

Our circuit of Sitia ended back in the square of Ayia Aikaterini, where the flower-decked epitaphios was positioned on its four legs in front of the door. The crowd jostled quietly in the outer dark as individuals waited their turn to stoop down and pass below the bier into the church. At this moment the left lens of my one and only pair of spectacles popped out of its frame and fell among the close-packed feet. I fully expected it to be shattered under someone's boots, or kicked away and lost forever among the dark stones. But when I knelt and put out my hand it closed immediately on the hard little shell of plastic. With a thank-you to St Jude and St Mathurin, I bent down in my turn and passed in among the lights and singing.

Later, down at the Ouzeri Mixos with a thimbleful of raki, I made friends with Andonis the pony-tailed owner and his chum Pericles. 'Come and have Easter lunch with us,' Andonis urged, sliding a pile of chopped apple onto the table between our glasses. 'We are having a lamb roasted on a spit.' I explained that I was on my way through to Zakros. 'Ah, well,' he said, 'they won't have a lamb like my lamb.' When I tried to pay for the drinks, Andonis made to give me a slap. 'No – from me. Kali anastasi; happy resurrection.'

On Easter Saturday I took a taxi down to Ano Zakros, the upland 'big brother' village of Kato Zakros which lay a couple of miles off by the sea. There were plenty of stares for me in the bar of the Hotel Zakros, where the old men of Ano Zakros were thumping down greasy playing cards and yawning prodigiously when they were not hobbling to the street door in order to hawk and spit into the gutter. It wasn't really a place for the stranger to hang out. I retreated to my room and got a handful of dirty clothes out of my backpack to wash them in the sink. No plug. Why hadn't I thought to bring one? I looked up 'plug' in my word-book. Confusingly for English-speakers, it was *tapa*. My request for a *tapa* at the bar counter fluttered the hen-coop, but a basin plug materialised at last. Back in the room I got out my plastic bag of soap powder. It seemed curiously limp, and there was a hole in the bottom. I looked in the pack; a blue and white snowstorm. I washed the clothes in the residue, rinsing out the gritty suds. Now to hang the wet clothes up to dry on my balcony. Oh – no washing line. Ah – no clothes-pegs. And no shops open. Here was a lesson, the first of many: think ahead. And stop sulking – it's really quite funny, isn't it? No? Oh, come on, Mr Grumpy, hang them up behind the door and have a sleep and get over it.

At nightfall the boys of Zakros ran through the streets throwing firecrackers, while their grandmothers rolled up and down the stepped alleys with bags of eggs and bread for the night's feast. Mrs Daskalakis, the owner of the Hotel Zakros, invited me to come to her house after the midnight church service for the family's Easter meal. Mr Daskalakis bought me a beer with a wordless smile. Towards midnight they escorted me up to the church where the bare-headed priest with his tightly rolled pigtail was performing hidden mysteries behind the painted wall of the iconostasis. Unlit candles were distributed among the congregation. Just before midnight the lights were extinguished, leaving the church in darkness. The face of the priest appeared in one of the portals, lit dramatically from below by the single taper he was holding. He turned and touched its flame to the nearest candle. Slowly the light passed from person to person, spreading ever more rapidly out from the centre until the whole church and the square outside were filled with soft radiance.

'Christos anesti, Christ is risen,' murmured Mrs Daskalakis to me, and I was able to dredge the proper response from the back of my memory: 'Alethos anesti – risen indeed!' I could have said anything, in fact, because at that moment the men and boys waiting outside lit the fuses of the firecrackers they had been saving and threw them in a deafening volley onto the forecourt of the church, where they spat and snapped like mad cats. It was the signal for an orgy of explosions. Whizzers fizzed across the sky, rockets went up with corkscrew trails of gold sparks, and out in the back country something was let off that boomed and reverberated in the hills behind the village like a naval gun. 'There are some crazies with dynamite ...' sighed Mrs Daskalakis.

15

Up at the house Mr Daskalakis marked a smoky cross on the front door lintel with his carefully warded candle flame. The family sat round the table with a few neighbours and we ate soup of rice, eggs, lemon and globs of stock fat, together with cold chicken legs and lamb cutlets. Mr Daskalakis's wine was very cloudy and very strong. After the meal we grabbed red-stained boiled eggs and attempted to smash those of our neighbours while retaining our own intact. Three-year-old Athi, the melt-in-the-mouth granddaughter of my host, ran out the winner by a mile. The roosters of Ano Zakros were already crowing the day as I entered my room at the hotel, full of egg soup and cloudy wine, and walked face first into my wet shirt. This time it did seem funny – bloody funny.

Mr Daskalakis himself drove me the last few miles down to the sea on Easter Sunday afternoon. Beyond the road the ground opened immense rocky lips to form the easternmost of Crete's many gorges. 'The Valley of the Dead,' Mr Daskalakis told me. 'We call it this because of many old tombs high up in caves in the walls. You will see tomorrow.'

Kato Zakros was a single strip of buildings – three or four tavernas, three or four rent rooms – on a curved beach of grey pebbles between headlands of rock. It was as muted and quiet as could be. I checked into a room and took final stock. It was pretty clear by now that I had planned the contents of my backpack badly. I could hardly lift it from the floor, and when it was up between my shoulders its weight crushed me forward into a kind of painful old man's stoop. There was no way on God's earth I was going to be able to carry it 300 miles up gorges and across mountains. A ruthless cull was the only solution.

The rejected items made a small but expensive mountain in the corner of the room. Out went my spare and heavier sweater, my jeans and my leather shoes. Out went my only T-shirt, my travel pillow, one of my two sets of thermal underwear. I tore out the pages I needed from my guide books and added the mutilated volumes to the pile; my collapsible umbrella, too. I considered sacrificing sun cream and survival bag, but thought better of it. Harmonica? No – too good an ice-breaker. Books – were they a luxury I could do without? I had only brought two, after careful thought: a paperback volume of the Psalms for day-to-day inspiration (I was going to allow myself 3 a day), and a copy of the *Odyssey* because I'd never read it and would need a real proper Greek hero to look to in times of trial. No: Homer and the Psalmist had better come along.

After lightening the pack, I felt lighter in spirit, too. I gave my inner poltroon one final pep talk. It's here now. Tomorrow you are going to be out there on the first step of the way with no GPS, no mobile phone, no Greek apart from a few bare phrases to save your neck, nothing to find your way through hard country with but a plain old compass and those shifty maps. Everything's exactly as you've imagined and wanted it to be. Let go of the idea that this is some kind of tough-guy challenge. If you want to bail out at any time, feel free. If there's an editorial voice still lurking in that downsized backpack of yours – the voice that says set the goals, get the story – ignore it. This adventure is not supposed to be like that. If you worry yourself by anticipating problems every day, you'll worry the whole walk long. Dogs? Sod 'em. Just take it as it comes. Go west, middle-aged man, and savour every moment.

Out East
(Kato Zakros to Kritsa)

'Blessed is the man that walketh …'

Psalm 1

At eight o'clock on Easter Monday morning I gave my boots a ceremonial dip in the sea, and selected a small pebble from the beach, grey and sea-smoothed, to carry with me for luck. Then I hoisted the pack and set off for the Valley of the Dead. The early April sun struck through the carob leaves, the sky was a stone-washed blue.

Near the entrance to the gorge a chicken-wire fence ran beside the path. Beyond it, dusty terraces rose up the hillside. A small hand-painted notice hanging by a dilapidated wire gate said, 'Minoic Palast Zakros'. The gate was locked, the whole place deserted. A large hole in the fence invited goats, dogs and passers-by to try their luck within. It was a characteristic introduction to a Cretan archaeological site – and the Minoan Palace of Zakros is one of the richest and best in an island laden with magnificent and still only half excavated treasures, an island that could well be styled the cradle of European civilisation.

⌐

Cretans developed their own version of their native history thousands of years before a British archaeologist named Arthur Evans began to excavate

18

a little knoll in the Iraklion suburb of Knossos at the turn of the 20th century. The Cretans said that mighty Zeus, chief among Olympian gods, had been born in their island, in a cave on the slopes of the Lasithi Plain, high in the Dhiktean mountains. His mother Rhea, pregnant with the unborn Zeus, fled from her spouse Kronos (who was also her brother), a God-awful monster begotten of a union between his own brother Uranus, ruler of the world, and their mutual mother Gaea. Kronos had castrated Uranus so that he himself could inherit the world; then, fearing a prophecy that he would be dethroned by his own son, the ogre ate the first five children that he sired on his sister Rhea. This was bad behaviour, even by the standards of the ancient gods.

In another cave under Mount Ida, Crete's highest mountain, baby Zeus was nursed by the goat-goddess Amaltheia. When he was grown, Zeus left Crete. He forced Kronos to vomit up his siblings alive and well, and together they succeeded in deposing their bestial father. Zeus became ruler of the heavens, and his two brothers took control of other spheres of Creation – Poseidon the Shaker, god of tempest and earthquake, held sway over the seas, while Hades governed the Underworld. But the chief god often returned to the island of his birth, generally in amorous pursuit of some lovely nymph or human girl. Zeus was immortal in the minds of most Greeks, but Cretans believed that he died and was reborn each year. In a somewhat puzzling twist, they also said that he was buried on the peak of Mount Iouchtas, looking north over the lush country around Iraklion and out across the blue Cretan Sea towards Greece and Mount Olympus.

On one of Zeus's visits to Crete he was accompanied by Europa, the beautiful young daughter of the King of Phoenicia. The god was in the form of a white bull, and Europa rode upon his back as he swam to the island. Once on Cretan soil Zeus reassumed his godly shape – or he may have changed himself into an eagle. At all events, somewhere in the south of the island, in the groves around Gortyn on the plain of Mesara, he had his way with his lovely companion. Of the three sons they conceived, one grew to be Minos the ruler, king in Crete, a man that some say was a just and even-handed monarch, others a bloody tyrant. Zeus loved Minos, and returned every nine years to the cave where Rhea had borne him for a conference with his son, patiently teaching him the arts of kingship. Minos had everything a king could wish for, including a complicated and wonderful palace which was built for him at Knossos near the north coast of Crete by the greatest practical genius in the world, the cunning craftsman Daedalus. To set the seal on his satisfaction, Minos's uncle Poseidon sent him a splendid white bull as a mark of approval. But the gods have a propensity to destroy those who become arrogant; and this gift had disastrous consequences.

If he had been wiser, or better-mannered, King Minos would have returned Poseidon's bull to its godly donor in the form of a sacrifice – the ultimate token of respect. But the Cretan king couldn't bring himself to destroy such a magnificent animal, and made the mistake of offering a lesser beast instead. Poseidon, mortally insulted, cast a spell on Minos's wife, Queen Pasiphae, causing her to fall hotly in love with the bull. The animal, however, showed no interest in her. Pasiphae secretly enlisted the help of Daedalus, who constructed a hollow model cow in which the queen concealed herself. The bull, inflamed by the beauty of the cow, mounted both model and hidden woman simultaneously. The offspring of this tragi-comic union turned out to be a freak, the Minotaur, with the body of a human and the head of a bull, whom King Minos ordered to be incarcerated in the mazy labyrinth of passages and dungeons that Daedalus constructed beneath his palace. Here the monster was fed on batches of youths and maidens shipped in from Athens.

Brave Theseus, son of King Aegeus of Athens, volunteered to join one of the consignments and try to put an end to the terrible toll of fine young women and men. On arrival in Crete the handsome young prince enlisted the help of Minos's daughter Ariadne. She gave him her heart, along with a ball of wool. Unravelling the wool as he went, Theseus entered the dark labyrinth, confronted and killed the Minotaur, and found his way out again by following the thread. The lovers escaped from Crete together with the other Athenian hostages, but after a night of passion Theseus

– not quite as honourable as he was handsome – abandoned Minos's daughter on the island of Naxos. To punish him, the gods caused him to forget to change the sails of his ship – the agreed signal that his mission had succeeded – and King Aegeus, watching from the cliffs, assumed his beloved son was dead and threw himself to his own death in the sea.

Back on Crete a furious King Minos was looking around for a scapegoat. Daedalus and his son Icarus fled the wrath of the king by flying away from the island on homemade wings of wax and feathers. High over the sea, Icarus became careless and flew too near the sun. The wax on his wings melted, sending him plummeting into the water. His grief-stricken father flew on to Sicily, where he went into hiding at the court of King Kokalos.

Those whom the gods wish to destroy, they first make mad. King Minos, crazed with lust for revenge on Daedalus – the architect, as he saw it, of the whole tragedy – was rash enough to follow him into the foreign island of Sicily. The daughters of King Kokalos attended the maniacal Minos as he took a bath, and there they scalded him to death.

∽

As a mythic backdrop to an island of strong passions and quick tempers, this bloody and fast-moving tale seems absolutely apt. Poking around the ruins of Zakros Palace that April morning, I thought of the gradual dawning during the 19th century of the realisation that there might be a historical foundation for the Gothic extravagances of these ancient world fables. The Italian archaeologist Federico Halbherr, shadowily remembered in Crete as a dashing figure astride a galloping black horse, initiated many digs around the island in the 1880s and '90s, discovering fragments of towns and dwellings and their artefacts that had lain under the fields and hillside rocks for thousands of years. But it was Arthur Evans's epic excavation from 1900 onwards of the palace of King Minos at Knossos, focus of the whole splendid old story, that grabbed hold of the public imagination. Whether there had ever really been a King Minos, or a Labyrinth with a bull-headed Minotaur, was beside the point. Evans unearthed a giant complex of dwellings – more like a close-packed town than a royal palace, in fact – with workshops and ceremonial rooms, strongholds and halls, staircases and colonnades, complete with pottery, glassware, domestic fittings, cutlery, tools, jewellery, and beautiful, vividly executed frescoes. There was controversy about some of his methods, particularly his penchant for reconstructing parts of the palace on fairly flimsy factual grounds. No matter, thought most of the watching world. Evans's discovery flung the door wide open on the brilliant 4,000-year-old civilisation he named 'Minoan' after its best-known, if not quite verifiable, ruler. By their paintings and sculptures, their buildings and engravings, the Minoans stood revealed as a vibrant, peaceful, prosperous and life-loving people, dancers and musicians, traders and manufacturers of beautiful jewellery and pottery, worshippers of bulls and of the deities in nature, able to read and write long before any of their European counterparts, with a spiritual and artistic sensibility far in advance of anything that had been expected of so ancient a culture.

Where there was one Minoan palace, there must be more. So judged the archaeologists, native and foreign, as they combed the island during the early 20th century, looking for signs and wonders. Grand complexes of buildings were unearthed at Phaistos on the Mesara Plain near Gortyn, and at Malia on the north coast some 30 miles east of Iraklion. But the far east of Crete seemed fruitless ground.

Stylianos Giamalakis, an Irakliot doctor, was an avid collector of antiquities. It was a call to the sickbed of a farmer at Ano Zakros that brought Giamalakis to the eastern end of the island shortly before the outbreak of the Second World War, and he had his reward when the grateful patient offered him, as in a fairy story, three gifts of gold – a bowl, a bull's-head pendant, and a diadem depicting a goddess-goatherd. They came, the farmer said, from that flat place down by the sea where an Englishman had found some antique houses forty years before. Dr Giamalakis knew of an archaeological dig carried out on the coastal plain below the Valley of the Dead in 1901 by the British antiquarian David Hogarth, and he could see with his own eyes the exquisite workmanship of the three jewels. He gave the farmer everything he had in his pockets, and added his gold watch.

The 'finds' were priceless treasures of the Bronze Age, at least as fine as anything that Evans had dug up at Knossos, and they pointed clearly to the strong possibility of another wonderful palace lying hidden under the olive groves and terraces of Kato Zakros.

With the war came German occupation of Crete, and archaeological activity shut down for the duration. Afterwards it was slow to get going again, but in 1962 the Greek archaeologist Nikolaos Platon began to excavate only a few feet away from Hogarth's old site. Immediately he struck a set of ruins which, as the dig widened out, revealed themselves as belonging to a palace of around the same date as Knossos and the other unearthed Minoan palaces, roughly 1900–1700 BC. Here were state apartments, bedrooms fit for a king and queen, treasury rooms, bathing halls, kitchens, workshops, cisterns, paved roadways. But there was one crucial difference. Zakros was far more complete, far richer in artefacts, than its sister sites. Unlike the other Minoan complexes, the ruins of the magnificent palace at the eastern end of Crete, it appeared, had lain undiscovered, undisturbed and unplundered ever since the Great Disaster of 1450 BC.

No-one yet knows exactly what caused the destruction of all the big town-like palaces at that late Bronze Age stage. Everyone is agreed that they had all been felled simultaneously some 250 years previously in a catastrophic earthquake. The archaeological evidence is quite clear about their destruction around 1700 BC, and their subsequent rebuilding in even more magnificent style – the hallmark of a vigorous and confident society. But what epic disaster could it have been that struck Crete in 1450 BC, levelling every palace in the island? The one common theme is fire, which scorched the stones and tiles at every site. An earthquake such as the one in 1700 BC would have trapped people in large numbers in the ruins, but there is no sign of that having happened. A tidal wave, perhaps? There was a huge explosion around this era on the volcanic island of Santorini, less than 80 miles to the north. A massive tsunami might have overwhelmed the north coast palace of Malia and the one at Knossos just inland. Zakros in its coastal position in the east could have been vulnerable, too. But Phaistos, ten miles inland in the sheltered south of the island? Most unlikely. And wouldn't a tidal wave have swamped and extinguished all fires when it hit? The eruption of Santorini, anyway, almost certainly happened many decades before Crete's disaster.

The finger seems to point to some man-made catastrophe, probably an uprising in the island which saw the palaces and other main buildings burned by rioters. Perhaps the insurgents were Myceneans from mainland Greece – they were well established in Crete by then, and subsequently took over from the Minoans, or at any rate lived alongside them. But could the participants in a raggle-taggle rising really have caused such damage, such crushing and flattening of solid stone buildings, of large, complicated structures? Or had that been simply the work of time? Whatever the truth of that ancient cataclysm, it spelt the sudden and complete end of the Minoan civilisation in its full flourishing. The secrets of those fabulous, expressive people sank underground and stayed hibernating there, stumbled in upon from time to time by robbers or lucky chancers, to re-emerge after some 3,500 years in all their butterfly glory.

I climbed the ancient roadway up the hill to a vantage point from which the whole palace of Zakros lay spread out for inspection – the dark eye of the circular cistern, the square shapes of the royal apartments, the great central court with its well where the excavators found a jar of olives that had lain perfectly preserved by the water for 3,500 years. Anyone who has strolled round Knossos with its reconstructed buildings and frescoes might be forgiven for finding the other Minoan sites of Crete baffling or even boring, unlabelled and at shin height as most of them are. But here at silent Zakros the mind's eye could conjure up, from previous visits to Iraklion's superb archaeological museum, the wonderful things so indicative of that Minoan love of life that were found among these ochre-coloured rectangles: ritual vessels of turned stone with gracefully curved handles, pigeon-chested jugs patterned with bamboo leaves and floral swirls, a *rhyton* or ceremonial ewer fashioned in the semblance of a bull's head, another made of exquisitely carved rock crystal with a handle of crystal beads stained a delicate green by the copper wire on which they were threaded. I descended the roadway and stepped out through the hole in the fence with a head full of marvels.

'Dead's Gorge' said the notice by the path. I crunched over sheets of pebbles brought down the gorge by last winter's floods, and entered the narrow mouth of the Valley of the Dead. Birds whistled and flew from dark caves high in the gorge walls where the Minoans buried their dead long before the great palaces were built. Signs of spring were everywhere – hard little green fruits on the fig trees, bird nests in the rock crevices, wild sage and thyme sending out their aromatic message. Scraggy sheep browsed among the oleanders with a donging of neck bells. Yellow-flowered asphodels rose from stony beds, and down on the floor of the gorge grew dragon lilies, the most sexual of plants, each large shoot resembling a slim pointed dog's pizzle sheathed in a crinkly-edged vulva of deep velvety purple. As symbols of springtime and the risen sap they couldn't have been more blatant.

The path, very rocky and marked with splodges of red paint, climbed gradually through the windings of the gorge to reach the road a little short of Ano Zakros. As I walked into the village a car pulled up alongside. At the window grinned the face of a Frenchman I'd spoken to about my expedition in Kato Zakros last night. 'Je suis Le Tentateur!' he hissed melodramatically, twirling an imaginary moustache and jerking his thumb towards the passenger seat. 'Va-t-en en arrière de moi, Tentateur,' I riposted, firmly if ungrammatically, and watched him roar away, his free hand making the sign of the devil's horns out of the window.

In Ano Zakros a battered tin E4 sign tacked to a telegraph pole pointed me on up a rough, rubbly path, an old *kalderimi* or cobbled track engineered centuries ago for transport by donkey. This was my first proper taste of conditions underfoot that would persist from end to end of the limestone island and wear the soles of my boots quite flat over seven weeks of tramping. I dug the figwood katsouna into the pebbles and skittered on up. At the top of the hill the path led out into stony and spiny uplands, gave a couple of wriggles and made off through a gate – a proper Cretan field gate, a square of metal rods filled in with chicken wire, hinged with wire and fastened with a wire loop to a lopsided opening in the fence.

These rustic gates, just sturdy enough to deter a sheep, were a feature of the Cretan countryside that I soon came to look for, their rusty orange materials hard to spot against the rust-red rocks. Beyond the gate the path, marked with sun-faded E4 signs, wound among the grasses of the sweet green valley of Skalia, side by side at first with a broad dirt road, then gradually diverging until the two routes vanished over the skyline several hundred yards apart.

Notwithstanding Le Tentateur, here was my first temptation. The map told me (I had not yet learned to treat the map with deep suspicion) that both ways would bring me to Ziros, the village where I hoped to beg a room for the night from Charis Kakoulakis's friend Mr Kharkiolakis. Was I going to give in this early and follow the dirt road with its implications of safety, its likelihood of a passing pickup truck? Or would I trust E4 to lead me through a lonely area where I'd quickly be in trouble if I turned an ankle, where I could get worryingly lost if the signs and poles ran out? I thought that if I didn't face the challenge now, in the not-too-formidable hill country of eastern Crete, I'd be slinking on dirt roads and looking for asphalt all the way. So it was a comforting twirl of the stick, and off along the thread-like path that lay beaten by sheep hooves into a dry orange strip among the spiky bushes.

A tiny wayside church came into view beside a scummy cistern. I went in and found lamps burning before an icon of a long-faced Virgin. The frame of the image was loaded with gently tinkling strings of *taximata*, tin squares stamped with legs and arms, eyes and hearts, youths in smart school uniforms, playfully kicking babies – symbols to reinforce prayers for afflicted body parts, for family members in trouble or joy, for a longed-for child. It was a continuation of an ancient tradition. The Minoans, too, had offered clay taximata to their gods in caves or in sanctuaries at the peaks of mountains. The tiny, crudely made models of dogs, babies, male and female genitals, heads and limbs, together with other statuettes of slim-waisted figures praying in a backward-bending attitude with the right hand pressed to the brow, are one of the staples of Cretan archaeo-logical museums, somehow retaining their mysterious force even when confined in a glass case. Here in the lonely church the metal *taximata*, uncomplicated symbols of the faith of their successors, held power, too.

The path ran past the empty pens and locked-up *mitata* or cheese-making huts of Zakathos, a seasonal settlement still waiting to receive the lowland shepherds who would soon be settling themselves up here to tend their sheep and make cheese all summer long. The E4 waymarks had been consistent enough, but now they melted away. Did the path go down that rocky defile to the left, or did it bend to pass beyond the bluff over there to the right? I looked at the map. No help. I got out the little field binoculars that Jane had given me as a parting present and scanned the ground ahead. Looking for six-inch-square scraps of faded yellow and black against a predominantly yellow and brown landscape is quite a challenge, I discovered. I was to get good at it before the journey was done, but this first day out my eyes and brain still needed too many clues. Sod it – go right and hope for the best. Ten steps more, and a decapitated waymark pole suddenly appeared among the rocks just ahead as if someone concealed there had sneakily poked it forth. The binoculars had swept over it a dozen times, but the eyes had failed to spot it. I stumbled on from pole to pole, trying to sense rather than see the way, letting my gaze slide over the jumbled landscape to pick up as if by osmosis the general line of the path. It was like trying to reach the image concealed in one of those computer-generated 3-D patterns, defocusing the eyes and looking beyond the psychedelic scribbles to the jungle animals or beach babes hidden within. Jane and the children had all been able to manage this without any effort from their very first attempts, but it was something I'd never been able to do. Now I found that trust was generally repaid with a sight of a section of kalderimi or a curl of identifiable path ahead. It was my first intimation that Map-and-Compass Man might have a kernel of intuition, even of common sense, somewhere about him.

At last I crossed the dirt road as it came looping in from the north. Now I had something to fix to the map. Soon enough the huddled flat roofs of Ziros appeared in their fertile valley far below. It was a great moment of relief and satisfaction. Between the Scylla of a dog on a long chain and the

Charybdis of a donkey with a nasty kicking habit I descended the path into the village, some seven hours and ten miles out from Kato Zakros. If that was going to be my rate of progress here in the easy hinterlands, what on earth would it be once I got into serious mountain country? Just as present, with the prospect of tilting a cold bottle of Amstel to my lips in the foreground, I didn't give a rap.

How stupidly accustomed an Englishman becomes to speaking his own language around the world, forever confident that some courteous elderly person or bright kid will materialise and be only too glad of a bit of free practice. In monoglot Ziros, a big back-country farming village very much absorbed in its own doings and a long way from any tourist trail, no English-speaker was forthcoming. I rummaged for my home-made phrase book and prepared to dive in. No rent-rooms, I'm sorry, said the village priest from his seat at a tin table outside the kafenion. The rooms are closed, confirmed the girl who brought the coffee. Rooms at Papagianades, maybe – ten kilometres that way, gestured the village grocer. Certainly I know Mr Kharkiolakis, said the tractor driver. Certainly he has rent rooms, but they are closed now. Ah – you are a friend of his friend Charidimos Kakoulakis. These rooms can be opened, then. No, Manolis, excuse me, but they are shut. No, Father, excuse me, but Kharkiolakis will open them. So much of the conversation I gathered through hand slap and arm wave.

The room above the Kharkiolakis taverna was typical of dozens of other village rent rooms I was to stay in over the coming weeks – quite spartan, quite featureless, clean enough, cheap enough, with cold water in the tap and hot bright sunshine out on the balcony. As I sat down on the hard bed I realised that the clip on my belt was empty. The Dog Dazer was gone. It must have twisted itself free somewhere in those wide uplands. Some shepherd would find it; what would he make of it? Would he press the button, and then puzzle over the sudden tail-between-legs flight of his canine companion? For me it would have to be the katsouna and a shout of 'Pare ta skilia!' against all bogey-dogs from now on. I found I didn't really mind. It was only a bit of kit.

Later a fit of the blues felled me. The taverna failed to open. Out in the streets of Ziros the shops stayed shut. The unshuttered house windows framed tableaux of families round dining tables loaded with meatballs, with stuffed vine leaves, with cheese wedges, with floury loaves. I was hungry. I couldn't speak to anyone. My washed clothes were wet, my unwashed ones stank. My room was cold and dismal, its electric light both weak and harsh. By its chilly pale glow I sought comfort in the words of the Psalmist, and was cheered in a sour sort of way to see that he was in a state of self-pity even more pathetic than mine as he ranted against the heathen. 'The ungodly are like the chaff which the wind driveth away,' he raved. 'Thou shalt break them with a rod of iron; thou shalt dash them in pieces like a potter's vessel.' That was the stuff to give the troops. 'Arise, O Lord; save me, O my God; for thou hast smitten all mine enemies upon the cheek bone; thou hast broken the teeth of the ungodly.'

Odysseus was in poor form, too, when I turned to him – a wandering, stormbound stranger in strange lands. A good read about someone else's troubles was as good as a feast. I went to bed on an empty stomach but in a better frame of mind. Out in the dark the occasion Eastertide explosion made the village dogs bark near and far. Other sounds in the midnight hour: mournful singing on a crackly radio, the clonk of sheep bells from some pen, and down by the reservoir a tremendous *jabba-jabba-jabba* as all the frogs in Ziros let their love come tumbling down.

Next day dawned cold and fresh. Along the road in Chandras there were no E4 signs to be seen. In the kafenion, already full of cigarette smoke at eight in the morning, I drank a short, thick, intensely sweet coffee. 'Papagianades? Along the road to Etia and then turn right, you can't miss it. What, *walking?* Well ... if you really mean it, then I would head for the windmills on the hill, and then – well ....' I followed the pointing fingers and came to a line of wind turbines at the crest of a ridge. Here at last was a proper forward view, huge and inspiring, ten miles west to the crumpled walls of Orno Oros and of Thriptis, the first of the four mountain ranges over which E4 was said to travel. I gazed on them and felt my heart lift, an actual physical sensation of pleasure and elation.

People were feeling good this morning. In Papagianades a woman gathering herbs by the roadside made me accompany her home so that she could fetch a bag of sweet cheese pies from her Easter stock. She handed them down over her balcony with, 'Sto kalo – go to the good!' Yes, exactly. I was trying my best to go to the good, but map and E4 signs were once more doing their best to frustrate me. Down in Vori, an untouched little hamlet of close-packed houses along needle's-eye lanes, an old man had blocked the street with his pickup while he unloaded firewood. What he told me about the path was in local dialect so strong I could make out only one word: 'Epano! Up!' But his pointing forefinger left me in no doubt. From the fantastic tangle of dirt roads on show in the valley below I was to select the one that would bring me up into the Oros foothills beyond.

For the foreigner, and especially for the walker, Cretan dirt roads are a hydra-headed puzzle. Since the 1980s and the universal advent of the pickup truck they have proliferated a thousandfold. Everyone wants to bring a dirt road to their hill village or their vineyard or cheese hut, and most applicants have been successful. Some dirt roads have subsequently been tarred, but most remain surfaced only with earth and stones – squidgy rivers of mud in winter, boiling funnels of dust in summer. Unsignposted side turnings to olive grove and vegetable garden, all identical to the main drag, are legion. Compass work on these murky byways is useless, because wherever you strike a dirt road you can be sure that within a mile it will have thrashed around through 360° without giving a clue to its ultimate destination. I did what I could to worry out the way, descending three times to the floor of the valley, each time ignominiously sweating it back up the hill into Vori's main street to be met with the steely gaze and uncomprehending head-shake of the old man. Didn't he have anything better to do than spend all morning unloading his wretched wood? Evidently he thought I was doing it on purpose. At last he grabbed me by the arm, quite crossly, and stabbed his finger forcefully at the mountains. Epano! Epano! Up there! Kat efthia! Straight ahead!

To escape from the social embarrassment of having to meet my nemesis again, I retraced my steps to Papagianades and hitched a lift with a fishmonger. A voice inside me piped up: 'Hey, that's cheating, Mr So-Called Solo Walker!', but I quelled it with ease. Not so my terror on the drive to the coast. The fish-man drove more furiously than Jehu, son of Jehoshapahat, frequently gesticulating with both hands off the steering wheel, while he harangued me about Kosovo. Beel Cleenton! NATO! Like Nazis! Yes, I temporised, expecting to meet death head-on round every hairpin bend – it's truly terrible.

～

The prospect of war in the Balkans had formed a stormy backdrop to my Cretan adventure ever since I had begun to think seriously about the expedition. After the ending of the disastrous and bloody Bosnian war in 1995 – either a civil war between ethnic factions in Bosnia, or a wider battlefield involving Bosnia's neighbours Serbia and Croatia, depending on where your political standpoint lay – the world's attention had switched to the republic of Kosovo, squeezed between the south-western border of Serbia and the north-east border of Albania.

Both Serbia and Albania had long-rooted claims to the territory of Kosovo. However, expansionist aspirations on the part of Serbia – the major component of the Yugoslavian federation of republics during the post-war half century that Communism held sway in the region – had been curbed, under the rule of Yugoslav President and strongman Josip Broz Tito, by granting a great measure of autonomy to Kosovo. The republic had its own political assembly, national bank, police force and university, and was largely controlled by the ethnic Albanian Kosovars who formed the majority of the population.

In the years preceding the fall of the Yugoslav Communist system in 1991, tension had grown between the Albanian Kosovars and their ethnic Serb counterparts, who accounted for only 10% of the population. Serbs in Serbia came to believe that their Kosovar cousins were being 'ethnically cleansed' by Kosovo's Albanian majority. In 1989 a new strongman leader, Slobodan Milosevic, emerged in Serbia and became President. He oversaw a crackdown in Kosovo against the ethnic Albanians, which its victims and critics viewed as a form of ethnic cleansing in itself. Political autonomy was abolished and a state of emergency declared 'to protect Kosovar Serbs from the Albanian majority'. Yugoslav state troops and police became responsible for law and order in the republic, and there were curfews and arrests along ethnic lines. Most of the lecturers and all but a small handful of the students were expelled from the university of the capital city, Priština. Albanian language newspapers, TV stations and radio outlets were shut down or heavily censored. Serbians took over the state-run companies, and over 100,000 Albanians lost their jobs. Soon four-fifths of Albanian Kosovars were unemployed.

It was a situation bound to lead to angry reaction once the binding glue of Communism had melted away from the mutually mistrustful republics of the Yugoslav federation. The Kosovo Liberation Army (KLA), an organ of Albanian Kosovar resistance, began guerrilla attacks on the security forces and civilian Serb residents of Kosovo in 1996. At the same time, international pressure grew on Serbia to call a halt to the ethnic cleansing of Kosovo. The Dayton Accords, the treaty by which the Bosnian War had been ended the year before, had not addressed the situation in Kosovo, and now things there got much worse – especially after Slobodan Milosevic became President of all Yugoslavia in 1997. The following year engagements between Serb forces and the KLA escalated; there were stories of Serb police brutalities, of the killing of women and children. Warplanes from the North Atlantic Treaty Organisation military alliance (NATO) began making flights along the borders of Serbia as a show of power in response to Serb army operations against the KLA there. The KLA itself began capturing new ground, provoking Serb incursions that brought rumours of massacres of civilians and prisoners. By September 1998 30,000 Albanian Kosovars were homeless, with the fierce Balkan winter just around the corner. It was a tragedy speeding quickly out of control, and the outside world felt compelled to step in.

US Special Envoy Richard Holbrooke had chaired the Dayton negotiations, and now he was sent by US President Bill Clinton to Belgrade to confer with President Milosevic. Under threat of his country being bombed, Milosevic agreed to allow unarmed 'verifiers' from the Organization for Security and Co-operation in Europe (OSCE) to enter Kosovo. Their presence produced no restraint on either side, and by the end of the year fighting was worse than ever. 1999 began with the world's press reporting the violent deaths of forty-five Albanian Kosovars on 15 January in the village of Račak – civilians massacred by Serbian police, or KLA terrorists killed in combat, depending on the onlooker's standpoint. The incident was a catalyst. Within fifteen days NATO had announced its intention of bombing Yugoslav targets – a decision unratified by the United Nations. Peace talks between Serbs and Albanians were scrambled together at Rambouillet near Paris on 6 February, but after a month or so they ended inconclusively. On demand was a right of passage through Yugoslavia for NATO peacekeeping troops, which to the Serbs seemed like having to accept a *de facto* NATO occupation of their country.

To Cretans, historically the allies of Serbs against their sworn common enemy the Turks, the NATO position looked very much like aggression, if not downright imperialism – in spite of the fact that the island's parent country, Greece, had been a member of the organisation for nearly forty years. Many Cretans especially disliked the presence and influence of the United States in the Balkans. The USA had been a bugbear to Greeks in general since helping to instigate the undemocratic political coup in 1967 which left Greece internationally isolated under oppressive military rule for seven years; while Cretans in particular, with their island's history of invasion and occupation over three and a half millennia, have always had a fierce hatred of outside interference and of the idea of foreign troops on friendly soil. Now in the spring of 1999 their televisions were showing them nightly images of Uncle Sam at work in the background of the escalating crisis in Kosovo only 900 miles to the north, his fingers in every pie from diplomacy and humanitarian aid to military rhetoric and the provision of ordnance for NATO bombing planes. They were outraged when, diplomacy and the threat of the big stick having failed and the OSCE verifiers having been withdrawn from Kosovo, NATO bombing of Serbian targets began on 24 March, exactly a fortnight before

I touched down at Iraklion airport. Greek TV news is no-holds-barred when it comes to graphic reporting, and already there had been a plethora of horrific footage of bomb damage, shattered bodies and scattered lives. Bill Clinton had become Beelzebub Beel, the universal devil in the Cretan consciousness. As a very obvious Englishman, and therefore undoubtedly a supporter of US policy towards Yugoslavia, I found myself elected the fairest of fair game for every roadside harangue-merchant and kafenion pundit I had the misfortune to come across.

～

Down on the coast in Mavros Kolimbos I got free of the death-wish fishmonger ('Fuck Beel Cleenton!' was his valediction) and slogged it up the long and winding road back into the mountains. Orno Oros stood up before me, grey and craggy against stormy black clouds that had been mustering from the north. A hole like a sinister Tolkien-style eye, pierced clean through one of the summits, looked down on me as I climbed through cool pinewoods and banks of thyme where little square beehives hummed to themselves in haphazard rows. A cold wind began to blow. I took off my sunhat and let the wind dry my sweaty brow. Everything felt good, but vaguely ominous, as the afternoon storm gathered force in a slaty sky. It was a relief when the tight white sprinkle of Orino's houses came into view far above on their saddle of ground, gleaming among the peaks in a shaft of sun that snapped off like a spotlight as the first spits of rain began to toss around in the wind.

In the village taverna, just reopened after the winter, I watched the sluicing rain through steamy windows. It was cosy and warm in there. A single pot simmered fragrantly at the back of the range. I lifted the lid on a green vegetable stew. It looked and smelt fine to a hungry man with only a couple of cheese pies between him and yesterday's lunch. The woman of the house ladled out a generous helping, which gave a curious clatter as it met the plate. A dozen round objects rolled clear of the greens. Snails. You is or you ain't a snail fancier, and I sure ain't. To me a snail is purely a garden pest. I hadn't put one in my mouth since conducting a childhood experiment in the cabbage patch. But here and now, with my hostess looking on, I couldn't possibly baulk at them.

After smiling to herself for a few minutes at my unavailing efforts to smash the shell by tapping it with a spoon, the taverna-owner took my gastropod education in hand. Look! Just twist a prong of your fork round in this little bubble thing on top of the whorl, and the snail's foot will slide out of the hole at the other end – see? Then you just spear it and pull the whole thing out. OK? Well – sort of. It was a clever trick, but drawing the dark grey spiral out of its hole was horribly like excavating a giant bogey from a nostril. I had to swallow the image along with the snail. It was not as bad as all that. I unscrewed another. Better yet. I ended up clearing two big platefuls, and would have attempted a third if the son of the house hadn't come in to practise his English and cense the table with cigarette smoke.

It was as well that he did, since I now discovered the trumpet-major effect that boiled snails have on the human gastric system. I bugled both high and low. The lad informed me with plenty of pantomime that the taverna's lavatory was temporarily out of use. This was a bit of a problem. There are many practical aspects to long-distance walking in Crete that the traveller only becomes aware of along the way, and here was one. Even without snails, the change from an English to a Cretan diet has its inevitable effect, as does all that healthy exercise. Once enthroned, so to speak, certain other considerations arise. One is the proximity of one's hosts, only a few feet away on the far side of a thin plasterboard wall. Another concerns the vagaries of Greek plumbing. Lavatory pipes in rural Greece tend to be of a diameter too narrow to allow the passage of anything as bulky and cohesive as paper. After a couple of episodes of failing to note the absence of the establishment's own paper until it was too late to alter course, I quickly learned to carry my own. A bin, however, is generally provided, and it is generally full of the 'cleaning materials' of previous occupants. Not necessarily the kindest influence on the senses. All these factors tend to combine to produce a state of increasingly uncomfortable egg-bondage in the recently-arrived walker. I paid extravagantly for an en-suite room in a hotel with modern plumbing on more than one occasion during the walk, solely to enjoy the pleasures of privacy and the relief of ... well, relief. In Orino this evening, though, it was a case of grip and grin.

Orino's rent room, unused since last summer, was a comfortless den. It was full of ancient cooking equipment, and it stank of damp. But the hot water switch proved effective, and once I'd got my sleeping bag spread out on the manky mattress I was happy enough.

At night Orino lay lit by a handful of twinkling white lights. Compared with the harsh lights that dominate the cities of north-west Europe as if a giant has smeared orangeade across the sky, the street lamps of Cretan villages look beautiful against the velvet black mountainsides. Up in the flanks of Thripti the stars shone perfectly clear in their millions, pricked into a night sky on whose horizons no city spread even the faintest of glows. I strolled up to the village phone box and put in my nightly call home. What a shock and a rush of joy as Jane gave me news I had never expected to hear. Some weeks before, I had sent off a collection of my poems to the Rockingham Press, in that mood of defensive resignation in which unpublished poets offer up their oft-rejected works yet once more to the judgement of yet another faceless editor. Now, said Jane, Rockingham had replied to say they'd like to publish the whole collection.

I had been writing poems for several years with intense delight. In the midst of producing books and articles for a living, I found acute pleasure in shaping and refining those tiny, pungent pieces for myself alone. What makes a poet? Writing a poem? Writing a *good* poem? Is a published poem more valid, better in some way than one that stays in the writer's drawer? I didn't exactly know why I wanted others to read what was so absolutely personal to me. But I floated back to that stinky old rent room on a very sweet cloud, and turned in with Homer. Telemachus, son of Odysseus, had quarrelled with his mother's boyfriends and was off in a huff, looking for his father. Great stuff to go to sleep on, one way and another.

'I am weary with my groaning,' keened the Psalmist to me in the morning. 'All the night make I my bed to swim; I water my couch with my tears.' Spot-on, as he very often turned out to be on my journey. I don't know if it was rats or mice banging the cupboard doors and dancing in the water tank, but their party row woke me with a jerk in the middle of the night. The only way I could shut them up was by switching on the ceiling light. Unshaded and glaring at some tremendous wattage, it shone mercilessly into my face, throwing a pattern of veins as red and branched as coral onto the back of my closed eyelids. I got up, turned it off and fumbled back into my sleeping bag. Bang, bang, scurry, crash, bang. I got up, switched on, got back into the bag. Silence, and the hot red glare in my eyes. I shoved in some ear-plugs, got up, switched off, crawled back between the covers, closed my eyes, tried to think of something nice – the poems, Jane, the kids, the starry mountains. A muted scampering, a muffled bang. The unmistakeable sound of tiny incisors gnawing, not far away. Extremely close, actually. In point of bloody fact, right beside my plugged ear. Out with the swearwords, on with the light. It was a long night. Orino's cockerels are early risers. Then rosy-fingered dawn did her bit. But at least her advent at the window meant I could put the light out. A couple of hours later I woke with a jerk, remembering I had to cross the Thripti mountains today and needed an early start. On the rent room floor and on my sleeping bag, shiny and black, lay the oval-shaped calling cards of those nocturnal party animals.

I filled my water-bottle at a tap fixed among ferns in the base of a tree, then followed the dirt road out of Orino. The east end of Crete is far drier than the west, but even in these mountains there are unexpected pockets of fertility. I passed one half an hour into the day under a great rough mountainside, a narrow plain where terraces of vines and vegetable plots mounded into lazybeds were all running and trickling with water. The irrigation pipe had split. It must have lain like that for many weeks; the spray of water jetting out of the crack was falling in a miniature wetland of bright green grass, ferns and mosses that it had itself created.

The morning was all uphill. On this kind of relentless ascent, gentle though the gradient was, the heavy pack forced me down to a dogged, first-gear plod. But with every piece of level ground, no matter how short,

I would find second and then third gears engaging at once, as if stored-up energy had been pushing at the lid of the box all the while. The dirt road thrashed about, climbing and climbing, leading at last to a breathtaking view from up on the heights of Afendis Stavromenos. From here on the roof of the Thripti range at nearly 5,000 feet, the prospect forward over the slim seven-mile-wide 'wrist' of eastern Crete took in two seas – the Cretan Sea to the north, caught in the surf-edged scoop of the Gulf of Mirambello, and to the south the milky blue Libyan Sea where Chrisi island floated like a water horse fifteen miles off in the haze. West across the plain the bulky grey massif of the Dhikti mountains rose 7,000 feet, its peaks white against the blue sky. The birthplace of Zeus was still capped with winter's snow. Gazing at it across twenty miles of country, I wondered how soon I would be there and how difficult its passage would be. The Thripti range, at all events, so large and impressive when I had viewed it from the ridge above Chandras (was that really only yesterday?), seemed to have shrunk under my boots and passed by almost unnoticed.

An hour later I was down among the fields of the mountain settlement of Thripti. People who had spent the winter down on the coast in Sitia or Ierapetra were beginning to drift back to the mountains to spring-clean their houses and fields. Many of the house doors were still closed with the 'Thripti lock' – a vine twig pushed through the handles. I watched a ragged-jacketed man pruning his vines while his wife in blue headscarf and black boots laid open the soil with muscular swings of a mattock. The vine terraces were buttressed and given shape by walls of huge stones, some sloping at alarming angles. At over 3,000 feet above sea level these were the highest terraces in Europe, someone told me later in the journey. They could be extremely old, too; terracing in Crete is an art that goes back to Minoan times. Thripti is the driest of the island's four mountain ranges, and its terraces make the most of whatever soil is available by allowing roots to dig further down to the moisture of the underlying rock. The terrace walls themselves reduce erosion by holding the soil together, and they make use of the stones that would otherwise be cluttering the fields and impeding the plough. The walker lucky enough to have time to stop, stare and ponder generally comes to realise that traditional methods of Cretan land husbandry, at first sight impossibly costly in terms of human sweat and effort, almost always turn out to be the best and most economical way to do the job in a particular location.

Manolis Xenakakis was rotavating the plot opposite his taverna. He shouted for his wife, and she came down from the roof, cigarette in mouth, to prepare me a brunch of souvlaki and salad, the rural taverna staple. A tumbler of Manolis's sharpish, cloudy red went with it; then another. I ate and drank in the cool dark room, serenaded by the house band of soprano flies and the occasional percussive sneeze from the dogs snoozing outside. Lethargic beasts, Cretan dogs, when they are not raving at you from the end of a chain. After the meal I went on, slowly, following occasional E4 signs along the dirt road that began an endless succession of hairpins as it zigged and zagged down the west face of Thripti beside the crack of the Monastiraki Gorge, a fearsome cleft full of indigo shadows that only a few intrepid cavers had ever managed to traverse. Stray stones lumped continuously under my boots, and the dust rose thickly. By the time I got down to the valley floor I was hot in the face, whacked to the wide and seeing double. The nearest hotel would do just fine. Flopping face down on the bed and sliding down the slope of oblivion in mid-afternoon seemed the most delicious of decadences. I'd have to watch that village wine at lunchtime from now on.

That evening the televisions on hotel walls and kafenion counters showed terrible images. The NATO bombardment of Yugoslavia had been going on for three weeks now, initially with the aim of destroying the country's air defences and major military targets. A thousand aircraft were reported deployed; Tomahawk cruise missiles were seen flying into bunkers and barracks. Serbian forces in Kosovo had responded by stepping up their aggression against Albanian Kosovars. 300,000 refugees were already said to have fled west or south across the border into Albania or Macedonia – though the Serbian take on this exodus was that the refugees were actually fleeing the bombs of NATO. Now, so Greek television was reporting with a certain air of injured self-righteousness, there had been a murderous catastrophe in Kosovo. NATO planes had attacked a convoy of refugees south of Djakovica by mistake, and had killed more than seventy of the very people they had sworn to protect. If the pictures shown on television were anything to go by, the planes had made a very thorough job of it. A tractor driver dripped in his cab, a smoking heap of chopped meat. Decapitated corpses sprawled. Babies lay blackened. These were images far more graphic than any I had ever seen. Customers commented vehemently on what they were watching. I did not want to raise my eyes to encounter anyone else's, and soon left my kafenion seat and returned to the hotel.

The grandfather of the owner was still pottering about. He invited me courteously to sit with him and his wife for a little conversation. I deployed the phrase-book until my thumb and forefinger were tired from riffling the pages. Albania, said the old man – I was there. Recently? No, no – during the war, fighting the Germans. 'Many mountains,' he said, 'much war. And now ...' I waited for it. 'Amerika in Yugoslavia! Bombing Belgrade!' He slammed down his fist among the glasses. 'Poof! Boom! All *epano* – blown up!' He grasped me quite gently by the hand. 'Why?'

I fumbled out the phrase I'd learned for just this occasion. 'Polimos ... foveros. War ... it's terrible.' Then I went to bed. There didn't seem anything else to say. If there was, the Psalmist was the man to say it. 'God is angry with the wicked every day. If he turn not, he will whet his sword; he hath bent his bow and made it ready. He hath also prepared for him the instruments of death; he ordaineth his arrows against the persecution.' Wasn't that a first-class description of NATO in the run-up to the bombing? Yet hard on its heels came: 'He made a pit, and digged it, and is fallen into the ditch which he made. His mischief shall return upon his own head, and his violent dealing shall come down upon his own pate.' Beel or Slobodan? It was hard to say. One last thought occurred before sleep: Cretans seemed quick to condemn the entire World of Beel as exposed on TV news, but were quite happy to watch, applaud and nod their heads in admiration at the spectacle of Beel's countrymen screwing, taking drugs and beating the crap out of each other on Hollywood film sets immediately after the news bulletin was over. Exactly like the rest of the world, then.

Before sunrise next morning I was sitting on a block of stone, greasing my boots for the day's march and listening to a bird in a bush singing *Siga-siga-siga!* Slow down ... slow down ... slow down ... Here at Vasiliki, idling by the Minoan house among pink spears of Cretan ebony, the temptation to laze away the morning was strong. Half buried in the ground behind me was a tight nest of deep rooms with walls two feet thick, small enough to cross in a couple of strides, interconnected by low arched doorways. Some of these basement rooms still showed patches of the pale red plaster that the house-builder smoothed across their walls more than 4,000 years ago. Other dwellings and lesser buildings lay spread across the hillside round about. When the site was excavated at the turn of the 20th century, among the ruins were found some of the finest examples of the potter's art ever unearthed in Crete. This 'Vasiliki ware', at its most striking in the form of tall jugs with spouts pointing upwards like the beaks of startled birds, had been semi-fired to produce mottled swirls of iridescent colour in red, black, brown and orange – a marvellous stroke of artistic achievement by its early Bronze Age creators.

The Red House must have been a luxury residence in its day, the country villa of some grandee of the early Minoan period before any of the great palaces were built. Whoever the owner of the Red House may have been, he commanded a wonderful view east across the valley to the great dark split of the Monastiraki Gorge, north to the sea in the Gulf of Mirambello. But his house came crashing down in flames around 2,200 BC, and lay hidden out of sight and out of mind while kingdoms rose and fell, invaders came and went, and cultures flourished and crumbled in the island over the next 4,000 years.

I sat on until the cocks of Vasiliki had crowed the sun up over the rim of Thripti, then walked up through the village where mules were being unloaded in front of the taverna, through the olive groves and on along the red dirt road into the hills. E4 signs led me into a wide upland of rocks and spiny cushions of *astivitha*. In a silent valley where pale mudslides held ranks of young olive trees, a tiny church and a solitary mitato marked the still deserted summer village of Asari. Here, reaching out to poke a shard of pottery from between two stones, I discovered that my figwood walking stick was not in my right hand. Tomorrow night, with any luck, I would be walking into Kritsa, the village where I had been given the white katsouna several years before. How could I do that without a twirl of my talismanic stick? Not for the last time on this expedition, I retraced my steps to look for the katsouna, and found it hanging on an E4 sign where I had stopped for a drink of water.

As if sulky at being baulked of its prize, E4 began to give trouble once more. High in the hills the dirt road divided into three. No signs. I was getting a bit braver now, and spun a coin with a pleasurable feeling of fatalism. Left came up heads, right tails. The middle way ascended to a broad plain of pale baked mud from which four more tracks diverged unsigned. What now? Angry barking came from a farmyard below. An old dame hobbled out to see what the fuss was about. Here was my chance. 'Pare ta skilia!' I shouted. 'Kala, kala, they're good,' piped back the woman, beckoning me down to the gate with one hand while she whacked the dogs into submission with the other. What about the path? 'Epano!' she said, pointing up the trackless hillside. Up there, boy – get on with it, don't be a nancy! Her son emerged from the house. What's the trouble, mum? Oh, the path to Meseleri? He drew a map for me in the dirt. The track splits down there, see? Then again. Take the left one, then go left again, be sure to go left, OK? Then right. Then it's just follow your nose, OK? You'll be there in an hour at the most.

An hour later, descending a lonely valley into which I'm sure the farmer never dreamed I would blunder, I admitted to myself that I was thoroughly lost. E4, if it even existed in these parts, was pursuing its baffling course somewhere over the hills and far away. There were two choices: burst into tears and wait for the robins to come and cover me with leaves, or keep on down this track and trust to luck. It led me to the Monastery of the Panagia Vryomeni, deserted and peaceful among the pine trees. The faded frescoes in the church showed a Nativity, a Presentation in the

Temple, a Crucifixion, and over the north window a depiction of Jesus being laid very tenderly in the tomb by sorrowing friends.

A pause, a prayer and a sip of water in this sunny, silent place were as good as a dose of Dexedrine. I subsided onto the bench outside and had a good look at the map. E4 ran on from Meseleri to the next village, Prina, and then took a great 20-mile swing across the heights of Dhikti before dropping towards the high oasis of the Lasithi Plain. That was, technically speaking, the way to go. But I had spotted something else – a big blob of settlement a little north of Prina, labelled 'Kritsa'. I had friends in Kritsa, the Aphordakos family whom Charis Kakoulakis had urged me to look up. I hadn't been there for years, but every previous visit had been a pure delight. What was more, a thread of dirt road seemed to connect Prina to Kritsa, and to run on towards the northern flanks of Dhikti. From there it looked as if a dodgy footpath might be my lot until I should rejoin the main route on the Lasithi Plain, but whatever its state it couldn't be more unreliable or misleading than European Hiking Route E4. Could it?

I sat pondering. Jane's words murmured in my inner ear: 'You're not writing a guidebook. You don't have to stick to a plan. Follow your nose and enjoy it, why don't you?' All right, then.

Below the monastery I found a wire fence across the track, bound up with a pair of ancient pyjama bottoms. Trespass time. I clambered through, tearing my trousers, and went down on sore feet through the olive groves and on into Meseleri. Stop here for the night? I consulted my shoulders, smarting from the pack straps, and my feet, bruised by the constant jabbing of stones on the track. Still a few miles in the tank, they told me. I followed a brand-new tarmac road, shiny black, that had just been slashed through the hills, and came to the village of Prina and the Taverna o Pitopoulis. No, there are no rent rooms anywhere near, said Dimitri the owner. My spirits sank. His wife Katerina took a look at me. Of course you could sleep here, if you don't mind dossing on the floor. Mind? I could have kissed her. Outside, where the cool wind could blow away the reek, I dumped my pack and took off my boots with a sigh of relief.

Dimitri worked his olive groves and vineyard, it turned out, while

Katerina ran the taverna. They had three children, and little money to spare. A few coaches brought parties of foreigners to the Taverna o Pitopoulis, but Prina remained out of the rich jetstream of tourism. Maybe the new road would make a difference. Prina, they said, was a typical Cretan hill village with an ageing population, pleasant to live in, but steadily losing its youngsters to the lure of seasonal tourist work in the nearby coast towns of Ierapetra and Agios Nikolaos, or to the college courses, brighter lights and better long-term job prospects in Iraklion or Athens. Recently there had been a few economic problems in Crete connected with immigration by Bulgarian and Albanian economic refugees. Their son had asked about several jobs in Ierapetra after leaving school, but all the positions had already been filled by Albanians. Bulgarians were hardworking types, keen to fit in socially – but the Albanians, well ... Still, one hoped for better days, didn't one? Make the best of what you've got, that's the trick, no?

It turned into a great night. There was no bar TV, and therefore no talk of war in Kosovo. A German couple pitched up after dark in search of a meal. Can you show us some vegetarian options? 'Ochi! No!' expostulated Dimitri. A meal without meat – what is that? Nevertheless, rumbling like a subsiding volcano, he produced a gigantic salad. Then the raki bottle was planked down on the table. Out came Dimitri's *laouto*, a beautiful old deep-bellied instrument with a fretboard inlaid with mother-of-pearl. We all had a go, and I discovered that the four pairs of strings were tuned like those of a mandola, an instrument I had hacked around on for years. Better still, a G key harmonica was one of the items I had retained during the Great Backpack Purge at Kato Zakros, some 70 miles back along the way. We made the dogs of Prina howl – something they scarcely needed encouragement to do. Dimitri abandoned the laouto to his guests and went out for his lyra. His stubby worker's fingers, one of them bent from an ancient dislocation, flew along the lyra's neck as he cradled it on his knee, the three strings keening against his fingernails, the short bow sawing back and forth in his other hand. My Greek was still far too embryonic to allow appreciation of the single-verse mantinades he sang. One featured a *monopati*, a footpath, and also a *dromos*, a road, and from Dimitri's winks and nods in my direction I took this to be a compliment to the sore-footed stranger within the gates.

'For the oppression of the poor,' said the Psalmist, when I sat on a rock just outside Kritsa to consult him the following afternoon, 'for the sighing of the needy, now will I arise, saith the Lord; I will set him in safety from him that puffeth at him.' An enjoyable image to take with me, as I gave the katsouna a good stout swing and limped down the hill into Kritsa.

Upcountry Village:
Kritsa Interlude

'The lines are fallen unto me in pleasant places; yea, I have a goodly heritage.'

Psalm 16

We sit under Argyro's tree, eating oranges – young and old, women and men, children, dogs and cats. Everyone in Kritsa knows Manolis and Argyro Tzanakis, and everyone in the place is bound to come down the road and into the Tzanakis garden sooner or later, for Argyro is one of those entirely open-hearted people around whom village life and social interaction revolve. Argyro sits in the leafy shade with a basket of oranges in her lap, a plastic bowl of potatoes on the table beside her, peeling and peeling, dispensing advice, lending an ear, giggling, commiserating, upbraiding. Scribbling opposite her, I imagine that the whole world will eventually drop in on Argyro for a cup of coffee or a glass of sweet spring water, if only one waits long enough under the lemon trees. I am trying out lines for a poem, one of a run that began back in Orino. It is as if the news from Rockingham Press has kicked open a blocked-up door and all these ideas are coming charging through.

Although I arrived yesterday my feet still ache, and I have carried out a damage inspection of them. Left foot: bruise under little toenail (now blue); abrasion above Achilles tendon; blisters on inside front heel, on ball

Argyro peeling oranges

Under a lemon tree Argyro peels
oranges. Friends encircle her, leaning
from blue chairs. Her little sharp knife pares
circlets of oily skin. Lengthening curls

of gossip swing. Efficiently she snips
the pitted ends, strips white pith, laughs
like a young girl. Now the talk digs
down to the pips. The black knife chops,

segments split onto the wicker tray
to sweeten talk. Argyro rocks and nods,
peels and shares, glancing from face to face,
her tongue-tip in her lips, calm as a tree.

of foot behind second toe, on outside of big toe. Right foot: bigger Achilles abrasion (strip of Compeed plastic skin on this); four separate rub-marks round ankle; blisters on ball of fourth toe, on tip of third toe. Both feet rather shiny and red. Soles: yellow carapace forming, goat-scented, rubbery to the touch.

I open my paperback book of psalms to see if the Psalmist is in tune with my mood of lazy contentment. He is not. In fact his poem for today is an absolute torrent of self-abasement. 'I am a worm, and no man; a reproach of men, and despised of the people. All they that see me laugh me to scorn: they shoot out the lip, they shake the head ...' He finds himself beset round by strong bulls of Bashan, ravening like lions with gaping mouths. 'I am poured out like water,' cries the wretched man, 'and all my bones are out of joint: my heart is like wax; it is melted in the midst of my bowels. My strength is dried up like a potsherd; and my tongue cleaveth to my jaws; and thou hast brought me into the dust of death.'

There have been mornings when I have felt like that, too, but not this one. I turn away from the worm in the dust and luxuriate in the smugness of sloth.

What a pleasure it is to have a shower that's warm and all-over, to wash all my clothes properly instead of dunking them in a cold sink, to sleep in a clean, sweet-smelling room. Why have I never properly appreciated this sort of thing before? What a delicious, guilty pleasure it is to have nothing whatsoever to do. Oughtn't I to be at my desk, at my computer, at my worrying and scurrying? I can't remember the last time I allowed myself just to waste a day. And here I am, doing it. Better not even look at what that stern moralist the Psalmist has to say about the idle. He is bound to threatening me with being broken like a potter's sherd, or cast out in the dirt. I kick back, stretch and luxuriate in wicked idleness. There's plenty of lazing still to be done before I saunter into town this evening and check out who's around. There are friends I've been looking forward to seeing, first and foremost George Aphordakos.

⤶

I'd come to Kritsa five or six years before, at the instigation of Charis Kakoulakis. 'Big village, Christopher – friendly people,' Charis had said, 'and one very special man, George Aphordakos, a policeman, a runner of the hills. George will show you all places of the mountains. He is *aegagros*, a wild goat of Crete.'

Mountaineers are the epitome of the masculine hero in Crete, and they come in two dimensions. There is the traditional *palikare* or strongman champion with a great black beard, his chunky figure encased in tight black shirt, capacious breeches and long leather boots. You can see him in any village on fly posters advertising itinerant musicians. Such men love to present themselves in this image, slung about with bandoliers, one fist enveloping a lyra, the other doubled on their hip, a *sariki* or fringed head-band twisted about their fiercely-knitted brows, gazing heroically towards a mountainous horizon. In contrast stands the lightly-made, athletic aega-gros or mountain goat type, all sinews and hollows. He might not be able to fell a bear with a blow, but he can leap tirelessly from crag to pinnacle where your palikare would struggle and sweat to follow.

George Aphordakos is a classic aegagros. I am probably more of a *vouvaloi*, a buffalo. Somehow we hit it off, to the point where George would take me out for long days hiking in the mountains from which I would return with scrub scratches on my shins, Pleistocene dwarf hip-popotamus teeth in my pocket and green ends to my fingers. George climbs mountains like the wind, pock-pock-pock from ledge to ledge, a hardback tome of Byzantine iconography in his hand, a flower book and a bird book in his pack. Out with George you pinch every herb you pass and sniff your fingertips, you truffle for fossils and Venetian frescoes, you grub up painted shards of pottery last seen by Minoan eyes. George's eagle glance picks out these things; his bony finger points you to them. When he has finished thoughtfully turning the rim of a 4,000-year-old vase in his hand, he gently reinserts it between the same two stones of the terrace wall from which he has retrieved it – such treasures, however tempting, belong to Crete, and are to be left in the field for the pleasure and instruc-tion of some future wanderer.

In George's company during that first sojourn in Kritsa, and despite the fact that his English vocabulary had consisted of two phrases – 'Problem!' and 'No problem!' – I had my antennae finely tuned, my eyes and ears well and truly opened. One day we climbed to the Dorian city of Lato, high in the saddle of twin hilltops a little north of Kritsa. By the time we had trudged the slopes of thyme, oregano, sage and rosemary, my hands smelt like those of a herbalist. 'Minoic!' grinned George, on his knees before a bush of wild olives growing in the shade of a wall. Cousin to the olives found uncorrupted after three millennia in the well at Kato Zakros, this primitive crop tastes tough and bitter, the thin little fruits hard to spot among leaves like slips of privet. Higher up we struck a cobbled kalderimi, which led to the gates of Lato. Walking between the massive stone blocks of the entrance and on up the stepped main street, glancing from side to side into the depths of grey stone rooms that sheltered olive presses, corn-grinding querns and cisterns unused since before the birth of Christ, I wished, as so often, I could speak better Greek. Later on in my travels around Crete I would learn the outlines of the island's wild and extraordinary history. But for now George Aphordakos, halting in the shrine of Artemis between the peaks and turning to me eagerly with a book in his hand and a whole mouthful of explanations, could only smile and shake his head in wry frustration before murmuring his catch-all mantra: 'Problem!'

～

When the palaces of the Minoans came crashing down in flames, it did not signal the immediate and final end of that sunny, life-loving civilisation. Whatever happened around 1450 BC – earthquake, tidal wave or insurrection – the Minoan way of life limped on. But the island of Crete, so green and fertile, so conveniently situated at the crossroads of trade routes between Europe, Asia and Africa, was always going to be a valuable prize for incomers who could summon the aggression and drive to take over. It was mainland Greeks from Mycenae who reoccupied the ruined palace at Knossos and dragged life and commerce in Crete back onto its feet. The Myceneans were a more warlike people than the Minoans; their dead were buried with swords and spears, and the designs on their pottery featured war chariots ridden by helmeted warriors – a far cry from joyful Minoan dancers and harvesters. The newcomers seem to have established a foothold in the island – perhaps as a servant class, perhaps as equals – for quite some time before the cataclysm. Now their influence spread throughout Crete as more palaces and towns were reoccupied. For a couple of centuries dominant Mycenean and decaying Minoan cultures uneasily coexisted. Then came the Dorians, efficient and well-organised fighters of Balkan origin who made a victorious drive south through mainland Greece and arrived in Crete from 1100 BC onwards. The Myceneans found themselves displaced, and the remnants of the Minoan people – sometimes called the Eteo-Cretans or 'real Cretans' – retreated with the rump of their language and their culture to the hills, where they may have hung on in decline for another thousand years.

With its shrines and temples, grand staircases, central courtyard and massive stone guard towers, the Dorian hilltop settlement of Lato was evidently more than a back country market town. In fact it was an autonomous city state, one of dozens that now established themselves in easily defended places within range of a sea port – Lato pros Kamara (present-day Agios Nikolaos) in the case of Lato. Gortyn was a great power in the south of the island, Kydonia (present-day Chania) and Polyrhynnia in the west, Praisos and Ierapytna (Ierapetra) in the east. Crete's city states warred and cooperated, feuded and forgave, made alliances and broke them, and traded as widely as they could across the Mediterranean. Pirates based themselves in the island, too, battening on merchant shipping out in the Cretan and Libyan Seas. During this last millennium BC Athens grew to dominate the Greek mainland, while Egypt remained the power in North Africa. Caught geographically between the two, Crete absorbed classical modes of architecture and sculpture from one, a starchy and formal Archaic style from the other. The fluid self-expression, the natural forms and individualistic styles of High Minoan art and society seemed a very long way off.

Enter the Romans in 67 BC, ruling from Gortyn and ushering in a period (as in Britain) of nearly 400 years of peace, prosperity and social stability, of temple-building, of theatres and forums, of villas and bathrooms, aqueducts and flush lavatories. As a captive on his way by sea to Rome, St Paul the Apostle made a brief stopover in the wild winter of AD 59, and a couple of years later his disciple Titus arrived to bring Christianity to the island. Roman rule began to run out of steam with the general decay of the Roman Empire in the 4th century, and it was the turn of the vigorous young Byzantine empire, spreading west like wildfire from its capital in Constantinople, to take over in Crete. By now the city up on the twin peaks and the high saddle of Lato had been abandoned; the humble port of Lato pros Kamara, formerly simply the commercial conduit of mighty Lato, had swollen to become a trading centre far better situated and more important than the old place back in the hills.

Unknowing

Shadowy, those Saracens, bequeathing
scarce footprints, light but cruel;
curved swords loosed from ships,
eagle noses savouring fresh blood,
scorched rafters.
      Why did they not
build, paint, sculpt in marble?
Pain and destruction: could these have sustained
a century of gold-ringed nobles?

Basilicas toppled, towns melted, a thousand
private or public Golgothas. Sum total
a blank; negative time.
      Then this grotesque
curtain call, the sky over Rabdh-el-Khandak
raining heads. Clipped beards catapulted,
eagle beaks broken on Byzantine stone;
what the modern mind grasps, barbarism
dealt to barbarians.
      Expunged, a slate
wiped clean. Folk devils fallen
out of retrieval into that desert of
dry dusty hearts we allot them,
unseeing, unknowing.

With one significant but obscurity-shrouded break, the Byzantines ruled Crete for almost a thousand years. They started by running the island's affairs with a business-like efficiency insisted upon by Constantinople.

Crete became a big agricultural producer and a far-and-wide trader. Christianity flourished in the round-apsidal basilica churches that sprang up all across the island. The rule of Byzantium seemed as assured as ever did that of Rome; but it could not withstand the great northward impulse of militant Islam when that phenomenon began to swell through North Africa and the Middle East during the 7th and 8th centuries. Arab Saracens invaded Crete from Alexandria around AD 824, driving out the Byzantine overlords and establishing an emirate in the island. And what then? According to tradition the newcomers slew thousands and pulled down the basilicas, including the great Church of Agios Titos at Gortyn after they had murdered its bishop Cyril. But modern historians are doubtful. The only fact everyone agrees on is that the invaders made their capital at the port of Knossos and named it Rabdh-el-Khandak, City of the Ditch – the city we know today as Iraklion. The Saracens used it as a slave market, and as a base for attacking shipping far out into the Aegean Sea.

The following century and a half lies cloaked in mystery. Looking back now, from a post-2001 perspective, the period of Islamic rule in the island assumes a resonance it did not carry when I walked through Crete. In the spring of 1999, reflecting on the regime of the Saracens, their actions and inactions seemed those of an alien civilisation whose motives, unless purely and absolutely mercenary, were incomprehensible. The Saracens appear to have destroyed much and built little in Crete. They left only a handful of coins to us – nothing of their art, of their architecture, of Arab culture. The Byzantines returned in 961 under their ferocious general Nikephoros Phokas to capture Rabdh-el-Khandak after a siege laden with every kind of savagery, including catapulting the heads of captured Saracens in among the defenders. Byzantine rule, once re-established, continued in prosperity for the next 250 years. Meanwhile the Arabs of Crete, and all they had done or failed to do in the island, slipped away down history's river of oblivion.

Limping on blistered feet from Argyro's house into town, I find the Aphordakos clan about its several businesses. In the years since I was last here Billy Aphordakos has transformed his simple kafenion into a youngsters' hangout quivering with brutal disco beats. Denim and leather hang heavy in the air. Lads slouch against their motorbikes on the pavement, posing for girls and each other. I have to pick my way over an obstacle course of crossed legs to get inside the bar. But this is nothing at all compared to the macho posturing in the north coast resorts of Crete where local bikers, fags in mouths, do wheelies all along the seafront with maximum noise and attitude. The boys and girls at Billy's are village kids, and politely point out the way to the Kafenion Kamara, the Aphordakos-owned café under the Moorish arch where I'll be bound to bump into someone I know. Tonight it's Iannis Siganos, the former mayor of Kritsa, bearded and forceful. He nods his leonine head, gives me a bear hug, orders *mezedes* and a little green flask of ice-cold raki.

'Well, Christopher, let me tell you ...'

It seems that Kritsa has been doing pretty well for a village of 2,500 inhabitants some miles from the sea. The 600,000 kilos of olive oil produced last year netted close to 400 million drachmas – something over a million pounds sterling. The *touristas*, Iannis says, are still turning up to buy the fine hand-loom weaving for which the village has a long-standing reputation. But it's seaside tourism that underpins prosperity in Crete these days; and Kritsa possesses neither beach nor sea, a terminal drawback in this sector of the economy. The villagers have had to do some lateral thinking and come up with an alternative enticement. Iannis and the other business heads of Kritsa have initiated a programme of local and agricultural tourism under the slogan: 'Come and see the REAL Cretan village!' Local families are being urged to encourage visitors to stay in their houses, accompany them to their work in vineyard and olive grove, eat at the family table, join in with the evening stroll and the morning marketing.

Kritsa, like almost every other Cretan town and village, is nervous about its future as a community. Can any of those youngsters hanging round Billy's doorway be persuaded to throw in their lot with the village, rather than drifting away to wait at table and clean hotel rooms in Agios Nikolaos, or take the plane for the bright lights of Athens and the wider world? Upcountry places, even those as big and lively as Kritsa, are suffering from a steady drain on their most important human resource, the energy and optimism of youth. The steady leaching away of young people from the country to the town isn't just a turn-of-the-millennium Cretan phenomenon, of course. It's been gathering pace all over Europe since the Industrial Revolution. In any case, bold young men and women have always struck out from their home villages for fame and fortune. Now, though, sighs Iannis as he refills his thimble glass and mine, it's as if someone has stuck a big needle in the heart of rural Crete and has been siphoning off our life blood. Maybe this 'Real Crete' thing will encourage some of our brighter youngsters to start a business here, raise their children in their home village. Maybe these computers will help, too. Who really knows? Anyway – as long as I have Katharo, I will stay sane, that's for sure.

The fertile plain of Katharo ('the clean place') lies 3,600 feet up in the Dhikti Mountains a few miles west of Kritsa. Most big villages of the Cretan lowlands have a 'mountain garden' high in the hills where they grow their vegetables, cultivate their nut trees and graze the sheep and goats on the spring and summer grass while they make cheese from the rich mountain milk. From Kritsa the rough road climbs some 2,300 feet to Katharo, and when you tip over the rim and descend into the lumpy, roughly circular plain in its cradle of mountains, it's like entering a green corner of heaven full of birdsong and the trickle of well water. So Iannis Siganos thinks, anyway. We leaf through the books of Cretan botany that he has brought along to the kafenion. 'You see this lily, this crocus, these white star flowers? All of Katharo! Oh, I love Katharo, my little house there, my garden. When I eat Katharo tomatoes, Katharo beans, it's something beautiful. There I can leave all my problems – breathe the air – be free! If I can live in Katharo all year, I would be happy. Ah, yes!' We bang our glasses on the table and chink them together. *Yia sou, Christophere! Yia mas, Ianni!* The emptied thimbles clash down on the tin table top, and Iannis tilts the raki flask once more while I select another olive from the dish.

Disgusting horrors from Yugoslavia flicker on the kafenion TV screen. There is certainly something to be said for showing these appalling things nakedly on television at the dinner hour if you want to bring home what war is and does. Iannis turns to watch. The Greek reporters employ measured tones as they reel off the places that have been hit – 'school ... houses ... hospital ...' Shots of roasted and disembowelled corpses, of head-scarfed women wailing in the rubble. Crying, shouting, denunciation and fury on the smoky streets of Belgrade. 'One can't have an operation like this without some mistakes being made,' remarks a US spokesman. 'We are trying,' explains British Prime Minister Tony Blair, 'to stop those who are murdering and oppressing each other.' These statements don't go down too well in the Kafenion Kamara. The impression Cretans are getting is of NATO, not the Serbs, as the murderers and oppressors, heavy-handed bullies imposing their will and destroying fleeing civilians from god-like perches in the sky. 'Why?' asks Iannis Siganos passionately, driving his two hands together with a smack. 'Why is America here? Why do they want to push everyone down beneath them? I am not a hating man – but now, in my head, I am hating America.' He gives me a long look, exhales, and ends with a low growl of 'Beel Cleenton – *fascista!*'

Next day dawns calm. I go out for a walk, wielding the white figwood katsouna, and am stopped by the first old man who spots it. 'Poli orea, very beautiful!' he exclaims, and holds out his hand for it. He hefts it, inspects the curve of the handle and taps the end lightly on the ground, nodding his head slowly. 'Stergios,' he smiles, and goes on. I stand with dropped jaw. That stick was presented to me on an Easter trip to Kritsa five years ago, and the giver's name was indeed Stergios. How on earth could the old man know that? I examine the stick myself on the way back to Argyro's, but it carries no name. Is it the shape, the wood, the feel in the hand that so clearly spells out the identity of the maker to those in the know?

Soon the light thickens over the village, and it becomes fantastically windy. '*Phissaiee*, it blows!' exclaims Argyro, and writes the word in my notebook twice over: '**ΦΥΣΑΕΙ**/φυσαει'. It's exactly the noise the hot wind makes as it roars and whistles over the town. 'From Africa, bringing the Sahara to Kritsa,' Argyro mourns, shaking her head over the red dust that stains her newly washed sheets on the garden dryer. Big, tree-shaking blasts send stray papers and cushions into the air and make the olive groves hiss in a white surf of upturned leaves. Argyro's mother, wrapped in fluttering black like a prophet from the desert, hugs herself in a chair by the wall. Cats and chickens cower. Old men sit and grumble in the kafenia as war news flickers on the screens.

I turn to the Psalmist for comfort, but today he is at his most terrifying: 'Then the earth shook and trembled; the foundations also of the hills moved and were shaken, because he was wroth ... He rode upon a cherub, and did fly; yea, he did fly upon the wings of the wind ... The Lord also thundered in the heavens, and the Highest gave his voice; hail stones and coals of fire. Yea, he shot out his arrows, and scattered them; and he shot out lightnings, and discomfited them. Then the channels of water were seen, and the foundations of the world were discovered at thy rebuke, O Lord, at the blast of the breath of thy nostrils ...'

Winds and wars, thunder in the heavens, bloody bodies on the screens, hailstones and coals of fire. No day to be abroad. I pull up the drawbridge, fetch a blanket and crouch into a chair with a head full of monsters.

'If it rains,' says George Aphordakos, who turns up under Argyro's lemon tree in mid-afternoon, 'it will rain Africa.' George has learned a good deal of English since we last saw each other – a lot more than I have of Greek. He looks as lean, tough and self-controlled as ever. He shows me a close-up photograph of a tall plant with gracefully curled white petals, rising from a rocky bed. '*Lilium candidum*, Cretan lily,' says George, as if introducing a queen. It turns out that this lovely flower has not been seen in the Cretan wild for many decades. George has travelled 300 miles on foot to look for it. The moment he spotted it, he says with hand over heart, was something rare. Where did he find it? George makes the sign of the cross over his lips. He is not telling. But he waves a hand in the general direction of the Dhikti mountains, and gives a tight secretive smile.

With George is his brother Manolis, another friend and walking companion from my former days in Kritsa. The Bros Aphordakos are polar

Phissaiee

The cat fussed her kitten under my chair
this morning, licking it, yowling uneasily, though
all seemed well. Stormcrow in black, the old

woman came, wrapped to the eyes, fluttering:
bad news in black rags. The day
thickened, darkened. Then phissaiee

roared down on Kritsa; hot blast
pouring east from Africa over the town,
a prophet shriek out of the desert, raging.

Groves thrashed; green seas of leaves
hissed like cats, turning white eyes to heaven.
Dark dots flew, imps or birds, storm-driven.

Doors clashed, chairs scattered, tempers
grated like sand. Old men growled, watching
war on the screen, Balkan neighbours burn.

'Thunder in the heavens,' cried the prophet,
'lightnings, hail stones and coals of fire.'
Apocalyptic, as from a frescoed church,

these breaths of hell: sliced men, babies
cooked and smoking, mothers in flames. Kritsa
crouched, back to the wall; phissaiee

scourged eyes to tears. 'Then did I beat them
small as the dust before the wind,' the prophet
foamed, 'I cast them out, as dirt in the streets.'

All day the cat prowled, circling
the chair where I skulked, one of the
ungodly, bowed under a blast from heaven.

opposites. George is a delicately-strung and abstemious *aegagros*. Manolis with his big black brows and ruddy complexion, his barrel chest and shovel hands, is the very pattern of a *palikare*. Manolis stands as strong as a bull, with wrists like thighs from his job working a compressor drill. He is an open-air man, a great sleeper under the stars, a hunter of rabbits and partridges up on Katharo; a laugher and quaffer, a family man and a gentle man, easily moved to embraces, who every now and then reaches out and silently kneads my arm or pats my knee.

Gestures are crucial to understanding the tenor of a Cretan conversation. What is said can often sound furiously angry, the words spewing out in a torrent, the timbre of the voice suddenly rising and hardening in a manner that to an English listener would spell imminent trouble, a temper reaching boiling point. Non-initiates expect a punch-up to flare out at any moment. But here in Crete that's just emphasis. The gesture, or gesticulation, is what's all-important. Sitting the following afternoon in the Kafenion Kamara with Manolis, George and their friends and family, I pick up on two that I can't remember having remarked before. The first sees the speaker's hand, extended with fingers stiffened karate-style, brought down sharply to chop the table with a startling bang, then thrust out palm upwards towards the victim. Translation: 'Here's my point right under your nose, fool!' The other piece of body language is more complicated. The hands start wide apart, cupped with palms uppermost, before being swept round, forward and downwards in a semi-circle to join each other, fingertip to fingertip, in the orator's lap. 'Well, this is what *I* think – and what any reasonable person would think, too.' Admiring the drama of these bits of arm theatre, I have to admit to myself that, however good my Greek gets as I pursue my Cretan odyssey, I will never muster the bluster to enhance my own tatters of talk by employing either myself.

It is almost time to bid Kritsa goodbye. Pantelis Kampaxis, the fit young mountaineer from Iraklion, has phoned to say he'll be here bright and early in the morning. Pantelis has volunteered to guide me over the rocky highlands of Dhikti for a couple of days – the footpath shown on the map is a chimera, apparently, and he has assured me that I will never find my way alone in those remote parts. I have the uncomfortable feeling that Pantelis, a young aegagros if ever there was one, has summed me up after our brief encounter up the stairs in Dikeosinis Street, and has pigeon-holed my capabilities only too accurately. Tonight I have been invited to eat at home with Manolis, his wife Rula and George Aphordakos. Before that, I intend to spend an hour or so in the Church of Panagia Kera, rapt among its medieval signs and marvels.

～

By the beginning of the 13th century the Byzantine empire had over-stretched itself and was well past its sell-by date. Rotting from within, as the Roman Empire it had replaced had rotted nine centuries before, the vast Eastern Orthodox organisation – itself now under renewed attack by a resurgent Islamic movement – trembled on its bough, ripe for the plucking. In the event it was the Latin Catholic Christians of western Europe who got there first in the bloodthirsty, freebooting form of the Fourth Crusade. In 1204 the Crusaders, led by the Italian Count Boni-face of Montferrat, sacked Constantinople, and the Byzantine empire was carved up piecemeal. The island of Crete might have been thought of as the plumpest of prizes, but in the end it was sold by Boniface to the Vene-tians for 1,000 pieces of silver – a somewhat symbolic sum. To claim their prize the Venetians had first to remove the Genoese, who had stepped into the power vacuum in Crete and taken over the island in 1206. It took four years before Crete was wholly controlled by Venice. The island was to remain under Venetian rule for the next 450 years.

In the 13th century Venice was an immensely powerful city state, keen to extend its arm far across the Mediterranean Sea. Crete proved an excellent forward base for trading, a handily-placed naval centre for dealing with the pirates who plagued the Mediterranean, and a rich source of prod-ucts such as oil, wine, corn, fruit and timber. Venetian adventurers and entrepreneurs were granted estates throughout the island, and they ran them in a feudal manner under the overall control of the Doge, who ruled from Candia (as the capital known to the Saracens as Rabdh-el-Khandak, and to the Byzantines as Khandakas, was now styled). Though the new overlords established a settled social order and a flourishing commerce in the island, they were by no means popular with the islanders, a tough mongrel breed with native Minoan, mainland Greek, Roman, Byzantine and Arabic blood in their veins. Perhaps owing to this rich mix of genes, the Cretans had evolved into a bloody-minded and independent people, not given to curling up and crying 'Master!' to anyone. Discontent soon took root among the islanders against the new taxes, penalties and feudal obligations imposed by the incoming Venetians on old Byzantine families and on the great mass of Cretan peasants. There were uprisings and rebellions – 27 major ones in all, and countless local 'difficulties' – during which a tradition of native raiding from mountain strongholds took hold. The Venetians responded by building fortresses down in the lowlands and on the coasts. After a great revolt in the 1520s the leader Kandanoleon, a man from the rugged Sfakia region of south-west Crete, was executed along with many of his family and followers. Such harsh treatment bred resentment. And there were external problems for the Venetians to worry about as well – namely, a great upsurge in the number and daring of Mediterranean pirates. In 1538 the Turkish corsair and admiral Khair ad-Din Pasha, 'Barbarossa' by nickname, sacked the north coast port of Rethymnon, causing the Venetians of Crete to strengthen the defences of their towns and cities against attack from the sea.

The Venetians were great and graceful builders in stone, and in the chief Cretan ports of Candia, Rethymnon and Chania they created harbours, forts and palaces of notable beauty. They also built hundreds of churches, all across the island, for the celebration of the Roman religion with which they tried to replace the long-rooted Orthodox faith embedded among the islanders nearly a thousand years before. Roman Catholicism became the official faith of the island, a state of affairs which many islanders could not accept and which bred yet more resentment against the usurpers. Sheer weight of tradition dictated that Orthodox worship continued in the cities where the majority of people followed the Orthodox faith. It carried on elsewhere, too. Orthodox priests approved by the Venetian authorities were supposed to be in favour of close ties or outright amalgamation with the Catholic church. But that was far from the general rule. It was all a hotch-potch and a bit of a bodge, and it meant that the Greek Orthodox faith, its monasteries and churches, continued to maintain a hold in Cretan hearts. This hold became much stronger during the 15th century, after the fall of Constantinople in 1453 to yet another resurgence of expansionist Islam, this time from Turkish roots. The Venetians of Crete, greatly (and justifiably) fearing the growing power of the Ottoman Empire, began to relax their religious restrictions on the Orthodox natives whom they realised they would probably need as allies against the common enemy.

Many cultured refugees from the Ottoman expansion on the borders of Renaissance Europe either passed through Crete or made their homes in what was fast becoming an outpost bastion of Christian civilisation. So Crete entered belatedly upon its own late medieval artistic and cultural Golden Age, a typically idiosyncratic and many-stranded one which mingled Catholic Renaissance sophistication, Orthodox Byzantine tradition and native Cretan earthiness and vigour. The literature of this Golden Age reached its apex early in the 17th century when Georgios Hortatzis published his tragic drama *Erophile*, still read and performed today, and Vitsentzos Kornaros of Sitia wrote his epic 10,000-line poem *Erotokritos* – verses of which you'll hear sung and recited with pride and pleasure by 21st-century Cretans of all ages. Painting saw its apotheosis towards the end of the 16th century in the religious subjects of Domenico Theotokopoulos from Fodhele near Iraklion, better known outside his native island as El Greco, and in the exquisitely figured icons of El Greco's contemporary Mikhail Damaskinos. Yet for my money the most wonderful of all these artistic riches of the Cretan Renaissance are the humblest, the commonest and the most accessible to the ordinary man – the gloriously colourful, lively and inspiring frescoes which embellish the walls and ceilings of hundreds upon hundreds of Cretan churches. Painters of icons, working within narrow conventions, found very limited scope for personal interpretation of their subjects. The Cretan artists who painted the walls of their little country churches in the time of Venetian rule felt no such inhibitions.

On my way down to the Church of the Panagia Kera on the outskirts of Kritsa I pass a man heaving along the carcass of a just-slaughtered lamb, its bloody head and hooves flopping in the dust – a reminder of Real Crete. Outside the Panagia Kera a coachload of French tourists has pulled up. They shuffle round the church, shepherded by a guide with a loud and grating voice. By dint of moving to whichever of the three aisles they are not occupying, I manage to have the impeccably restored frescoes more or less to myself. Before becoming immersed I take a minute or so to recall the Byzantine convention by which the biblical topics are arranged throughout the church: Christ Pantokrator ('All-Powerful') looking down from the ceiling of the apse, the Evangelists and Holy Fathers below him; in the roof of the nave, scenes from the life of Christ including the Nativity, Baptism, Crucifixion and Resurrection; the lower walls occupied by a selection of military and secular saints; on the west wall a depiction of the Second Coming of Christ and the ghastly torments of the Damned to terrify outgoing peasants at the end of each service.

In the central nave I find a calm St Michael dispatching a very lowly dragon, each of the beast's thorn-like teeth a single bold stroke of white paint. Salome in harlot scarlet balances the head of John the Baptist on top of her own in a dish with a beaded rim as she performs a wild jig in front of King Herod and his cronies. In a ferocious Slaughter of the Innocents a mother cradles in her lap the severed heads of three infants with the faces and receding hairlines of middle-aged men, while Mary and the infant Jesus hide in an annexe from a file of Herod's men who, dressed in Venetian chain mail and cloaks, are about to slice off the head of another baby. In the north aisle I stand a long time admiring a walled and fortified Garden of Eden where birds perch in the trees, the four Sacred Rivers curl from their springs like grey horse tails, and a bright red seraph with six wings and a spear guards a door at which the outcast Adam and Eve knock unavailingly. There's an action-packed Day of Judgement, too, in which the souls of the Damned, dressed in white jumpsuit-style winding sheets and packed one behind another into a communal tomb, go hurtling like a bobsleigh team down a dark rocky defile into Hell, where a crowned Satan with a snake for a scarf awaits them among his horde of demonic enforcers.

I drift across to the south aisle, whose scenes are dedicated to the Blessed Virgin Mary. A remarkably beautiful Virgin, large-eyed, sorrows with her hands outstretched in resignation or pleading. On a tiny donkey she journeys to Bethlehem, shielding her swollen belly with one graceful hand, a gesture completely natural. The most touching depiction of all is a highly emotional Sorrow of St Joseph. The indignant carpenter of Nazareth, hurt and betrayal all over his countenance, turns his back on his pregnant betrothed and hunches into the bottom corner of the fresco like a sulky child. An angel reaches out a comforting hand, but is ignored. Mary, tense and miserable, slumps in a richly carved chair, her head sunk on her palm. 'Oh, Joseph, don't do this to me … it's true, what I've been telling you! There's no-one else, honestly!'

All over the church one sees faces painted full of sorrow or joy, hands outstretched in admonition or sympathy. Actions generous and mean, loving and brutal are part of the warp and weft of human existence. Life and death contend, closer than brothers. In the background birds flirt and leaves shimmer, flowers deck the meadows, cloud shadows cross the sky, streams tumble, shelf-like mountain ledges pile upwards to rocky peaks. You only have to step outside and glance about you to see where these island artists found their inspiration.

The Plains of Plenty
(Kritsa to Asites)

'Hold up my goings in thy paths, that my footsteps slip not.'

Psalm 17

In two days I covered forty miles in the company of Pantelis Kampaxis. We crossed the northern corner of the Dhikti Mountains, traversed the Lasithi Plain and threaded the rough hills beyond. Far more ground was covered than I'd bargained for; and for most of the way, had I been on my own, I wouldn't have had a clue about the route.

I got an inkling about Pantelis's level of fitness as soon as we had left Kritsa. On the mountain road to the plain of Katharo we cut corners mercilessly, forging a straight line upwards across the rubbly slopes, only touching the road at its hairpin elbows. Under his skin-tight running shorts Pantelis's leg muscles bunched like steel hawsers as he sprang lightly ahead from stone to stone. By the time we had climbed 2,300 feet to the edge of Katharo I was a panting ball of sweat; but my companion's brow betrayed not one spangle, his chest nary a heave.

Katharo in the full flush of April was just as delectable as Iannis Siganos had promised. The new grass of the undulating plain lay spattered yellow with flowers. Fruit trees foamed pink and white. The first tractor of spring went grunting along a field, drawing a dark furrow in the soil, and a man walked behind, casting out seed by hand from a basket. Those fresco painters of the 16th century might have stared in wonder and terror at the red-nosed devil snorting and clawing the earth in front, but they would instantly have connected with the timeless figure of the sower and his deliberate tread along the furrow, the easy, strength-conserving swing of his hand and the silvery shower of the falling seed as it caught a glint of sunlight.

Head-scarfed and knee-booted Katerina had opened her little taverna for spring only an hour before we appeared on her threshold, but she bustled about to make us a cheese pancake and to set a jug of clear, earth-scented Katharo well water on a table outside. We ate to the sound of birdsong, and Pantelis offered me a few slices of his own story. He was happy enough working as a hotel bell-hop down on the coast, saving money in order to marry the pretty girl who'd accompanied him to our Dikeosinis Street meeting. George Aphordakos was his brother-in-law, he revealed, and together with the mighty palikare Iannis Pantatosakis they formed a trio who often went hiking, climbing and mountain running together – hence the Kampaxis thews and sinews. 'Iannis knows every stone of Crete,' said Pantelis, 'he is always in the mountains. Always.'

We followed the dirt road through the middle of the plain, looked down upon by a pair of snowy peaks away to the south. The lesser of the two was certainly Lazaros. The greater height, named Spathi by Pantelis, had the mapmaker's name of 'Dikti', the 7,047 ft summit of its namesake range. What do maps know? – particularly this equivocal specimen flapping itself to shreds in the sharp mountain wind. I had the measure of it by now with its misplaced villages, non-existent paths and economies with the truth of contours. If instead of 'Dikti' I had found 'Everest' printed there, I would hardly have raised an eyebrow.

At the west side of the plain a stony gully took us up to a saddle of ground spread with clumps of orchids and drifts of crocuses. 'Give a girl a crocus,' observed Pantelis, 'and you are saying something serious to her.' Here we pulled up to take a last look back over Katharo, the 'place of purity'. God forbid that a current scheme to attract a richer class of international *tourista* to the Kritsa area by building a first class golf course on the plain, complete with access highway and many-starred hotel, should ever come to pass.

Now the path – if there was a path; I never made out a trace of one – threaded one of those scrubby, rocky, up-and-down wildernesses I was coming to recognise as a keynote of the Cretan mountains. We began to gain height, moving steadily up through a scoop-shaped basin of ground. Massive old *prinos*, the spiny prickly oaks of the uplands that one finds grazed by goats into all manner of outlandish forms, clung to the rocks with gnarled fingers of roots. Rivers of birdsong poured from bushes and trees that had colonised the ledges of ancient, long-abandoned terraces. A rubbly old kalderimi ran round the rim of the valley, passing the ruins of a couple of cheese-huts as it climbed gently to the upper skyline. I asked Pantelis how long he thought it had been since people lived and worked in this silent hollow in the hills, but his reply was a shrug and a shake of the head. Who knows? A long time.

Looking back from the pass we had an unexpected and final glimpse of Katharo, a far green island among grey waves of limestone. Ahead, a thousand feet below, lay the patchwork fields of the Lasithi Plain, a perfect circle of perfectly flat ground within another bowl of mountains. A dozen villages were spaced out evenly round the perimeter. It was like looking at a relief map from an eagle's back. But where were the famous 10,000 'wind-mills', the little cloth sails in Maltese cross shape that once whirled round to power the irrigation pumps of the plain and keep Crete's picture postcard photographers in business? 'Not put up till summer,' said Pantelis, 'but they are very rare now.' Why was that? 'Electricity' was his one-word reply.

Descent to the plain was by a precipitous hillside of ankle-breaking scree. The backpack pushed me this way, swung me that. I had to dig in my Kritsa katsouna and watch every step like a hawk, while Pantelis the aegagros grew smaller and smaller as he leaped balletically down before me. Down on the plain at last, we stayed to pass the time of day with a shepherd whose local accent, even I could tell, was of the strongest. 'Hard to understand, even for me,' said Pantelis as we walked on, following the dead flat dirt road past the skeletons of abandoned wind-pumps.

Tractors raised plough dust from the fields each side. The dry plots made a strange contrast with the straight drove roads dividing them, which still gleamed silver with the undrained floodwater of winter, rich in the minerals leached from the surrounding mountains that form such productive soil in the plain. Lasithi was always a place of lush fertility, and also of refuge and resistance. After a rebellion in 1263 so ferocious that reinforcements had to be brought to Crete from Venice to snuff it out, the people of the plain caught the brunt of Venetian revenge. They were all evicted, their homes were destroyed, and for the next two centuries not a seed was permitted to be sown in the wilderness of Lasithi.

In the village of Psychro we stopped to shoot the breeze with a family, acquaintances of Pantelis's, who sat in plastic chairs by the roadside in hopes of selling a piece of weaving to a passing tourist. It was wonderful to get the pack off my aching back and sit behind a glass of raki and a cup of intense black coffee, with nothing to say or do except smile at Father (or perhaps it was father-in-law), the village priest in grey cassock and tall black stovepipe hat, his uncut hair neatly scrolled in a bun at the back of his head. He was the first to leap to his feet and cajole a party of French motorists when they pulled up for a moment.

At nightfall, with 20 miles or more under our belts, Pantelis and I pitched up at a cheap hotel – a cheerless place with cold water, a chilly room and a very nasty lavatory. I sat like a stone with aching feet and a nice big beer. 'I think I will go for a warm-down,' said Pantelis. His warm-down consisted of a 15-mile run – a *run* – right round the rim of the plain. 'You don't have a problem if we share a room?' enquired Pantelis politely on his return. Problem? I would have slept like a log if he had been an axe murderer with a very loud stereo.

In the night I woke to find the temperature had dropped below freezing. A shivery mountain night with a million stars above and a hard frost on the fields. Close by, hidden in the black slope just behind the hotel, the mouth of the deep dark cave in which celestial Zeus was born. Frogs jabbered in their hundreds from the ditches of Lasithi, and the village dogs kept them company with a concert conducted all over the plain.

Early mist was smoking from the ditches when we set out in a pink and pearl dawn. According to the map – but unacknowledged by any waymarks – we were back on E4 once more. Scarfed and swaddled women were already riding in pairs on the little potato-sorters as the tractors dragged them round the deeply furrowed fields. In the villages mules were being saddled and kicked into motion. A woman passed us with three goats on a lead, their muzzles wrapped in cloth bags to stop them delaying progress to the high pastures by grazing at the roadside. A causeway led above the *khonos*, the rocky gash which drains the plain of its winter floodwater. The khonos lay half choked with dumped rubbish, its sides embanked by neatly maintained stone walls. It was a long and (for me) sweaty slog to the top of the pass, but the view when we got there was even better than yesterday's over the Lasithi Plain – a great mouth-watering prospect west to the coastal sprawl of Iraklion and its fertile hinterland of olives and vines, climbing gradually inland to meet the noble profile of Mount Iouchtas, the summit where Zeus lies buried. Three eagles – Zeus's own birds in Greek mythology – were wheeling over the peak. Against the blue haze forty miles off in the west rose the long white spine of Psiloritis, Mount Ida of the ancients, the highest mountain in all the island. Its snow-covered flanks fell seemingly sheer, their sides indented with dark ribs of shadow. I gazed long and delightedly towards the roof of Crete. In a week's time, maybe less, I should be taking the final steps of the climb to its summit.

'Waiting for us to fall down,' commented Pantelis of the circling eagles; and in the ensuing couple of hours they might have picked my bones if my luck had been a little worse, or theirs a little better. The dirt road we were following, having dipped kindly at the start of its downward run, suddenly thrust its head into a solid wall of rock and gave up the ghost. Like yesterday, the only exit strategy looked to be a thousand-foot scramble down a pathless slope. But yesterday's descent was a doddle by comparison. This mountainside fell away at about 60° of slope. It was blanketed in prickly bushes and carpeted with slippery rocks that skidded and squirted away from under my boots. No waymarks, of course, and no visible path either. If E4 had been set by its 'planners' to snake down here, it was being very modest about it. I turned into a cowardly spider, a wobbly-kneed creeper and crawler. The pack and its unbalancing weight was the problem. That, and my clumsiness. And my general unfitness, my creaky knees, my cartilaginous twinges. And my chicken-heartedness. I began to despise my timorous self, doubling into a crouch to sidle round each step in the rock, as I watched Pantelis bounding on down far below. Clouds of dust marked his track as he skidded and cornered in his slick little trainers, exulting in his sense of balance, his young man's temerity. Every now and then he would stop and gaze back up the slope, hands on hips, the picture of aplomb as he assessed my progress. Halfway down, the inevitable happened; I tripped over the katsouna while Pantelis was watching and took a toss, sliding headfirst for twenty feet into a needly tangle of astivitha tussocks. Oh, bollocks. Physical damage negligible – a scratched arm, a bashed shin. Psychological bruises – painful. What was it the Psalmist had said, four or five days ago? 'I am a worm, and no man; a reproach of men, and despised of the people.' I can't say I caught Pantelis actually shooting out his lip and shaking his head, but I knew what he was thinking; and later on he admitted it. 'Christopher, when I saw your technique of coming down this mountain, I thought of how you will manage on Psiloritis and on Lefka Ori, and I was not happy for you.'

I was not happy for myself. I started down that slope a middle-aged man of forty-nine in good spirits. I reached the bottom two hours later a tremulous old pantaloon, shaking in every limb. 'Technique' – that was the word that really stung.

I was more than glad to limp along the road into Kastamonitsa and melt into a chair in a wayside kafenion. A fierce little coffee and several glasses of water brought back balance and perspective. I found I was even able to raise a smile at myself. After a restorative hour we moved along, a four-mile trudge on a good asphalted road, and entered the town of Kastelli singing and munching green almonds that we'd pulled from the roadside trees. We'd agreed to meet again a week from now in the village of Ano Asites. Pantelis, troubled about my solo capabilities, would make himself available to see me safely over Psiloritis and down the other side. Though foreseeing further bouts of humiliation by comparison, I was pleased to think he was going to come with me.

In Kastelli Pantelis handed over his knapsack for me to put on the evening bus to Iraklion, shook my hand politely, and ... yes, *ran* off there himself. After watching him sprint away down the street, I spread out the map and measured his route. Twenty-five extra miles at the double: taking the piss, or what? But that – I reasoned, settling down behind a cold beer and a plate of chips – that was your Cretan aegagros-style mountaineer for you. Humbling company, this brotherhood of lean men who watch their calories, exercise rigorously, take part in marathons, scorn cigarettes, drink sparingly or not at all, warm down instead of chilling out after a punishing day in the hills, and go to the stadium to train as many nights a week as their wives or girlfriends (if they have them) are prepared to put up with. Ho hum. That's why Pantelis strips off like an olive-skinned god, and I strip off like a milk jelly.

'Thou hast set my feet in a large room,' sang the Psalmist, turning his back for once on the broken potsherds and the coals of fire. 'Blessed be the name of the Lord: for he hath showed me his marvellous kindness in a strong city.'

Kastelli ('the Castle') was a sleepy little agricultural town sunk among vineyards and olive groves in the rolling country south of Iraklion. Farmers went buzzing through the streets by day on their *mikani*, motorised tricycle pickups that farted out toxic plumes of two-stroke pollution. The men of Kastelli came in at night to the kafenia round the main square for noisy sessions of backgammon and cards. Old women wrapped to the eyes in black hobbled through the streets, carrying on their backs their own bulk in green stuff harvested from their gardens outside the town. Goats bleated behind ancient wooden house doors in the narrow side lanes. It was just the place to recuperate by lazing a day away.

In the morning, delighting in soft shoes and a light day-pack, I hired Michalis the taxi-driver – black rumpled suit, wraparound shades, Ronald Colman moustache – to take me out to a hilltop a couple of miles away, where I had been told the ruins of the Dorian city-state of Lyttos lay. I had got well into the *Odyssey* by now, and had an idea of Lyttos in its pomp as a large and powerful place. Homer asserted that Idomineos, grandson of Minos and King of Crete, had managed to fill 80 black ships with men of Lyttos to go to the siege of Troy. Lyttos was a prosperous city, controlling a strip of the island which stretched from the north to the south coast and contained the fertile plain of Lasithi – a vital source of supply. Certainly the city-state was at war with Knossos from the 4th century BC onwards, and it had its claws out for other neighbours, too. This aggression rebounded on Lyttos during the war of 221–219 BC when, after launching an attack on Ierapytna (present-day Ierapetra), the men of the city returned home to find that warriors from Knossos had descended on Lyttos in their absence, wiped the place off the map, and decamped with all the women and children. Utterly devastated, the Lyttos men could not even bring themselves to enter the ruins of their city.

Lyttos was rebuilt. The city-state is known to have resisted the Romans on their invasion of the island in 67 BC, and it seems to have prospered for a good six or seven hundred years more. Today, poking around the overgrown hilltop, I found few signs of that vanished city. Two churches stood there, one dedicated to St George and the other to the Holy Cross, their walls partly constructed with stones from ancient Lyttos carrying fragments of inscription and beautifully carved acanthus leaves. Between the churches the hilltop was a riot of spring flowers – poppies, mallows, marguerites, vetches, treacle mustard in a spatter of scarlet, yellow, gold and white. Through screens of flowers and mats of hanging greenery, patches of coarsely squared blocks and rubble showed where the great defensive wall of Lyttos had once run. I sat on the stump of a Dorian column, basking in the sunshine and looking out east to the grey wall of Dhikti. With my binoculars I could distinguish the line of the dirt road from Lasithi petering out in its terminal rock face, and the slope down which Pantelis and I had come. How very easy it looked from here and now.

Idling back into Kastelli late in the afternoon I passed between olive groves scented with wood smoke. Under the recently pruned trees glowed

The olive fires

A football thumps the wall; young footsteps
skelter down the lane; the old man bleats,
'Yanni, Yanni.' His grandson scoots to other
mischief. If he had his way, those brats
would learn some manners. Drained by the long day's drift,
he sighs, yawns, marooned in easy weather;
prowls to the door, flicks his beads, unwilling
idler in calms, circling on boredom's raft.

All day a tang has hung about the town,
seeping downwind from bonfires lit to burn
dry olive prunings. Nosing the lobby air,
sterile and stale, the hotel owner's father
scents bitter sweat and woodsmoke from the bar
where old men in stained work clothes drink together.

lines of bonfires where the trimmings were burning. A man stopped me to touch and admire my stick with the by now familiar 'Poli orea! Very beautiful!' A flood of delight, one of those throat-catching, unfathomable surges of bliss that visit at rare moments, poured through me as I sniffed the olive smoke on the darkening road.

In a restaurant in town that night an enormously fat cook slugged on a bottle of Coke and puffed a fag as he prepared my (delicious) pizza. The place was all but empty, something I was grateful for when the cook switched on the TV to reveal a chaos of shattered buildings and screaming ambulances. NATO planes had hit the office of the main Serbian television station in Belgrade. Fourteen dead, many maimed, said the reporter through tight lips.

I sat late at a table in the hotel lobby, talking olive farming with the owner and his father, very pleased to discover that I had mustered enough Greek by now to keep my end up and maintain the threads of a conversation in my head. The older man – neat, tall, upright, his thick hair smoothed back – spoke courteously with the slow, carefully enunciated phrases of an educated man. I had seen him during the day prowling the lobby between desk and door, back and forth, back and forth, swinging his worry beads, occasionally sighing, fastidiously covering his yawns of boredom with a well-manicured hand. Such refined elderly men suffer excruciatingly from ennui in modern-day Crete, cut off from the cameraderie of their village contemporaries, the ordinary chaps who drink together and still get their hands dirty in orchard and field.

By eleven o'clock next morning, 23 April, I was sitting in a cell in Angarathou monastery, drinking raki with Archimandrite Stephanos Marankakis. Already that day I had seen a nasty road accident (an old man knocked over by a boy racer in Kastelli), and had eaten an on-the-hoof breakfast of sweet bread and new cheese pressed on me by church-going crowds celebrating St George's Day. I had covered the best part of 10 miles, too, blundering through gardens and following dead-end tracks on the bad advice of lying waymarks, being reminded all over again of the frustrations and farcicalities of European Hiking Route E4. But now, chatting with the vigorous old monk in a mixture of my minimal Greek, his two words of English and a tiny mutual store of German, our creaky talk helped along with sips of raki and nibbles of sweets and nuts, all was well.

Well now, how old do you think I am, eh? 21? Ha, ha, flatterer! Come on, have a guess. 65? No, more than that. 70? Certainly not! I'm 88, I am. Look, here's a photo of me during the war with my friends. Which one d'you think is me? That one, the handsome boy with the slim figure? How did you guess, eh? Ha, ha! Come along, have another drop of this raki, it won't hurt you. Walking? Excellent – raki will make you strong, make you into a proper *palikare*, like I used to be. Not now, alas. You beg to differ? Think I'm not quite ready for the scrap-heap yet? I agree with you! Life in the old dog yet, eh? That's right! Ha, ha, ha!

Dear old man with his white-rimmed eyes, his healthy ego and sense of himself, full of glee and gaiety. I left him waving at the door of his cell, calling out blessings and brushing cake crumbs from his long white beard. It didn't take more than half an hour to get myself thoroughly lost once more.

Angarathou monastery lay in semi-wild gardens thick with Cretan sage and drowsy with the cluck of hens and the murmur of bees. I took the tarmac road up to Sgourokefali, where it was washing day. Cylindrical electric coppers bubbled in front gardens. Among the green waves of trees the flat rooftops of the village streamed shirts and pants like a fleet of signalling ships. Beyond here the country rolled and dipped, its billows broken by green ravines with cliff-like sides that cut north across the grain of the land to reach the coast around Iraklion. The pale earth was studded with the round green buttons of olive trees lined up in ranks, and with rows of vines, some up on trellises, others free-standing. It was good, fertile, profitable farming country, and new grant-aided dirt roads to olive groves and vineyards had proliferated and intertwined in recent years like a nest of identical but equally untrustworthy snakes. Among them E4 occasionally raised a black and yellow sign, invariably in the apex of a fork. I chose a turning at random, and found myself after an hour looking up at the flapping underwear of Sgourokefali once more.

The village men were all standing under a tree, getting drunk in honour of St George with the help of a 20-litre box of paint-stripper plonk labelled 'The Party's Wine'. There were lots of firecracker explosions, and a none-too-friendly air about the shouts of laughter that greeted my enquiry concerning the path to Mirtia. One man took me to the top of his dirt road and pointed out the track that had just led me round in a circle. There, man, there! Like the old man back in Vori on my second day out, he just couldn't believe I could have any doubt about a route he knew all too well. I raised my hands and shrugged. Yes, but ... To placate him and show willing, I set off once more down the road and turned the other way when I reached the fork. Twenty minutes later I was slinking back through the square at Sgourokefali. The drinkers under the tree sniggered and shook their heads. In the end a man not quite as far gone as the rest fetched his three-wheeler mikani, loaded me into the pick-up part and put-putted me down to the fork in the dirt road. There he indicated an obscure green track that I hadn't even spotted. Along there to Mirtia! OK!

I crossed a ravine by a slender Turkish bridge and came up through Ano Astraki into Mirtia, where I asked for directions in a kafenion full of men even drunker than the tree-huggers of Sgourokefali. I won't even try to unpick what went wrong after that, nor how I came to a standstill at last on the brink of a hundred-foot cliff; let alone dwell on the many miles of uphill backtracking that had to be faced. It is wonderful how one's feet feel fine when the going is good, but every cut and blister opens up and screams when you're feeling sorry for yourself.

Back in Mirtia, one of the kafenion merrymakers seemed to be offering me a lift. Half an hour later I was still twiddling my thumbs. Then I caught him smiling slyly round his circle of friends and making a little contemptuous gesture in my direction. Good old rustic humour at the foreign boy's expense, eh? I phoned for a taxi and had myself taken off to the next sizeable town, Archanes, where there proved to be a rent room available at not too outrageous a charge. Cold water from the hot tap, and from the cold tap too. But so what? It was a roof and four walls.

In the taverna that night there was a sudden high farce panic with much shouting, wielding of brooms and hasty mounting of chairs. 'Zpider with poisoning,' said a fellow diner by way of explanation. I joined the chair-climbers. These alarums and excursions drove the name of Mirtia out of my mind; but later, picturing the place and the Turkish bridge I'd crossed to get to it, I recalled Mirtia's illustrious literary connection. It had been the family village of Nikos Kazantzakis, the 'Tolstoy of Crete', certainly the island's most famous and best-selling writer, a controversial figure whose novel *The Last Temptation of Christ* attracted widespread condemnation as blasphemous. The author of two classic novels set in Crete, *Zorba the Greek* and *Freedom and Death*, was born in 1883, when the island was still battling to throw off the oppressive yoke of Turkish rule. His early experiences of that archetypal Cretan life-and-death struggle for freedom shaped Kazantzakis's whole life and art, causing him to travel the world in search of a code of individual and spiritual liberation. This life-long journey brought him from revolutionary nationalism through sympathy with communism to an exploration of religion, and on out along more recondite philosophical shores. After his death in 1957, the Orthodox Church would not permit this atheist with strong religious impulses a burial in consecrated ground. So Kazantzakis lies buried in the ramparts of the Martinengo Bastion on Iraklion's city walls, facing Mount Iouchtas with its noble escarpment profile of Zeus. The writer's monolithic slab carries his simple statement of belief: 'I hope for nothing; I fear nothing; I am free.'

~

Like the Byzantines before them, like the Romans before that, the Venetians' rule in Crete reflected the drift of affairs in the parent state, gradually turning soft, rotten and ripe for the plucking. And like the Byzantines, it was yet another upsurge of expansionist Islam that brought about their downfall. The Ottoman Empire's capture of Constantinople in 1453 was a giant blow to Christian security, and equally a formidable boost to Muslim self-confidence. Pirate raids by Turks and Arabs became the scourge of the Mediterranean. Not for nothing did the authorities in Crete engage the greatest Venetian engineer of the day, Michele Sanmichele, in 1538 to strengthen with mighty bastions the walls that had been built around the Cretan capital of Candia the previous century on the foundations of the Byzantine city wall. Rethymnon and La Canea (modern-day Chania) followed suit, to mixed effect – Rethymnon was sacked and burned in 1567 by Algerian corsairs. But wall upon wall could not keep out the Turks when they finally launched their invasion of Crete in 1645. Under Yussuf Pasha they took La Canea in their first eastward push after a bloody siege of 55 days, and Rethymnon fell to Yussuf the following year. With Candia things went less easily. It took an epic siege of 21 years, with many thousands of deaths and countless unrecorded barbarities on both sides, before the gates of the city were finally opened by the defenders on 5 September

1669. The Venetians remaining inside were the last unconquered of their era, and were allowed by the Turks to leave in peace the now subjugated island they themselves had dominated, exploited, influenced and made their own for over 450 years.

What followed was, essentially, 230 years of decline and neglect, a period still seen by Cretans as the nadir of their island's fortunes. Feelings run very strong on the subject of Turkey and the Turks. The surest way to catch it hot, verbally if not physically, from a Cretan – a small town or village dweller in particular – is to utter anything that sounds even remotely like approval for anything originating east of Greece and south of the Black Sea.

Turkish rule was characterised by long periods of laissez-faire and navel-gazing. Minarets and domes were grafted on to churches-turned-mosques, beautiful fountains were built, Moorish window arches and wooden balconies were added to Venetian town houses. Thick sweet coffee, honeyed pastries and the pleasures of the *narghile* or hubble-bubble pipe were introduced, as was the affectionate diminutive '-akis' – Theodorakis, 'little Theodore', Kakoulakis, 'little Kakoulis' – that ends so many Cretan surnames. But it would be hard to point to any solid, sensible, hard-headed benefits of those two and a half centuries of Turkish rule. The everyday business of agriculture and trade did not seem to interest the new masters, urban by inclination and habit as they were. Pashas or overlords ruled the three districts into which Crete was now divided, and these officials and their minions tended not only to spend their time in the three main towns of Megalo Kastro (Iraklion), Rethymnon and Chania, but to dismiss the ever-worsening financial and agricultural problems of the countryside as unimportant. Lack of economic vision and purpose meant that the coffers of this naturally fertile and commercially well situated island – coffers that should have been full to bulging – were too often depleted, and the temptation for the Turkish authorities in Crete was always to top them up by increasing taxes on a population that could not maintain the prosperity necessary to pay these levies.

Given the independent-minded and combustible Cretan temperament, it is small wonder that the era of Turkish rule was punctuated by ferocious uprisings based in rural and mountain areas. These were always guaranteed to fetch the authorities out of their lethargy with a bang, and to trigger savage suppression. The leader of the 1770 rising in the west, a learned Sfakiot nicknamed Daskalogiannis or 'John the Teacher' who had counted in vain on Russian support in his struggle against their mutual enemy, gave himself up at Frangokastello Castle on the south coast and was brought for questioning in front of the Pasha of Iraklion. At first the Pasha treated the prisoner with courtesy, but when Daskalogiannis was bold enough to defy his captor he was taken out and flayed alive. The unfortunate leaders of some other rebellions were impaled, or dropped from poles onto boards stuck with meat hooks. Hatzimichali Dalianis and his followers were slaughtered wholesale at Frangokastello in 1828. Those who took up arms under the rebel leaders, and the people of the districts considered to have supported them, could likewise expect no mercy from a Turkish and native soldiery which gained itself a name for vicious behaviour, even in times of comparative peace. In the opening years of the 19th-century, for example, the French consul reported from Chania that the city's Janissaries – young Christian men who had converted to become elite Muslim soldiers – were casually shooting Cretan passers-by for fun, after making bets as to whether they would fall face down or up.

Urban and lowland Cretans who lived cheek by jowl with the Turks had to learn to get along with them. Mostly they did. There were large-scale conversions to Islam, some perhaps from sincere motives, many to ensure an easier life. But up in the back country and the mountains it was a different story, especially after mainland Greece broke free from the Ottoman Empire in 1832 after a ten-year war of independence. Emboldened, the islanders mounted rising after rising. In 1862 rebels fired the powder magazine at Arkadi monastery in the mountains behind Rethymnon, killing 2,000 friends and foes. The outside world began to take note and apply pressure on Constantinople.

The next uprising, that of 1878, was supported by Greece. This was the rebellion that formed the backdrop to Nikos Kazantzakis's greatest novel, *Freedom and Death*, with its ultimate palikare of a hero in Captain Michales, who goes down fighting for the glory and freedom of Crete along with the cream of his men. The 1878 rising ended with the establishment of Crete as a semi-autonomous state, and like those that followed in 1889 and 1896 forced more concessions from the Turks. As the Cretans sensed that their Turkish rulers were reaching the end of the road in the island, the four Great Powers of Europe – France, Italy, Russia and Britain – brought their diplomatic weight and the threat of their warships to bear on the Cretan rump of the tottering Ottoman Empire. In 1897 the Greek flag was raised on the hill of Profitis Ilias outside Chania in a protest organised by the man destined to become Greek Prime Minister and Crete's greatest political hero, Eleftherias ('Freedom') Venizelos. Its pole was shot away by the gunfire of naval units of the Great Powers at anchor in Suda Bay, but the Cretan patriots streamed the flag out manually and continued to fly it by hand, a bold gesture which brought spontaneous applause from the gunners in the ships. Finally in 1898, between diplomacy and threats, the Great Powers imposed a settlement. Unlamented, the Turks at last quit Crete.

That was not quite the end of the road, as it happened. The people of Crete did not only want freedom from the oppressive rule of the Ottoman Empire. They also craved *enosis*, or political union with mainland Greece; and the Great Powers were opposed to the idea, for fear it would provoke the Young Turks at that time revitalising the Ottoman Empire, and perhaps set all the Balkans aflame. Eleftherias Venizelos convened a Revolutionary Assembly in 1905 as a ginger group to push for *enosis*. Five years later he was elected Prime Minister of Greece; and three years after that, on 1 December 1913, the Greek flag was again raised in Chania, above the Firkas fort on the harbour. This time it remained proudly flying from its pole, a symbol of *enosis* achieved.

～

On the morning after St George's Day I got up early and did my daily washing in a cold and slippery stew of blue suds. This mundane operation, generally carried out at the end of each day's march, had been an essential part of the routine since my decision on Day One to sacrifice half the contents of the pack to the god of lightness. My total clothing commissariat now consisted of: 2 walking shirts, cotton, long-sleeved, with breast pockets to hold sunglasses and specs; 1 set of thermal underwear; 3 pairs of light socks and 2 of heavy walking socks (these now full of *astivitha* prickles inextricably interwoven with the wool); 2 pairs of trousers, washable, one torn at the knee and crudely stitched; 1 light sweater; 1 handkerchief; 1 anorak; 1 fleece; 1 pair of shoes, light, canvas; 2 pairs of underpants, post-pristine. A simple piece of hard-learned advice to anyone thinking of following in my footsteps – take dark-coloured underpants if you wish to avoid hotel balcony drying-line mortification.

My friend the Psalmist had his own, not dissimilar concerns today. 'My wounds stink and are corrupt because of my foolishness. My loins are filled with a loathsome disease: and there is no soundness in my flesh. I am feeble and sore broken: I have roared by reason of the disquietness of my heart ... I am ready to halt, and my sorrow is continually before me.'

Hmmm, yes. What else at this stage, roughly a third of the way into the walk? A plague of boils on my back, probably the result of sweating all day, every day into a shirt impregnated with the previous day's salt sweat, the previous night's unconditioned soap suds. Feet a bit of a mess, and stinking like a Psalmist's wounds, but negotiable with Compeed and cold water douches. Spirits fine. I wish, I wish, but it's all in vain; I wish I was a maid again ... or at least that I had prepared a bit better. Slopes, stones, screes – all were finding me out. On the plus side was the gradual acquisition of a tongue and the courage to use it. In the bank at Kastelli the girls had gathered round, smiling and astonished to hear the *tourista* speak Greek – not so much at its quantity or quality (I was still at the stage of recycling words or phrases picked up as I went along), as at the strange phenomenon of an Englishman making an effort.

Archanes offered two fine archaeological outings, the perfect excuse for a day off to let the sun get at my salt-stiffened clothes. I climbed the little hill just north of the town and steered for the ancient burial ground of Phourni, which looks out to the twin-peaked bulk of Mount Iouchtas. This is one of the most remarkable cemetery sites anywhere round the Aegean. So often it is luck as much as good judgement that drives our archaeological understanding. The Cornish fisherman shoots his net a couple of feet this way or that, and the corner slides across the golden cup from famed Atlantis. Manolis, feeling the need for a cigarette, climbs out of the ditch he has been digging and crushes with his boot a tablet of clay stamped with hieroglyphics that match those on the as-yet-undecipherable Phaistos Disc. So many accidents and happenstances to break the spinal cord of history; so many gaps to be filled in with educated guesswork. But at Phourni one sees a complete picture, an unbroken succession of Minoan burials, a millennium and a half that stretches from the early era, around 2,500 BC, down to the end of the Minoan age and the rule of the Myceneans after the destruction of the great palaces. All sorts of grave-goods have been found here: large clay *larnakes* or coffin-chests painted with vivid scenes of burial, bronze vessels, imported treasures including an Egyptian scarab, gold and silver jewellery, remains of a horse sacrifice, the skull of a bull, and a Minoan ossuary packed thickly with human skulls and bones. Several *tholoi* or circular tombs with vaulted ceilings stand on the site, those from earlier Minoan times containing multiple burials, later ones with single occupants.

I wandered among grey chambers of massive squared stones where burials in *larnakes* and *pithoi* (the classic large earthenware jar) had been discovered stacked up to 18 deep. Most of these chambers were close-packed to form the familiar Minoan nest or labyrinth of buildings, their compartments interconnected with doors, tunnels, passages, openings, other secret little rooms. Off to one side, near a big stone beehive-shaped *tholos* where the remains of a high-ranking priestess had been excavated, seven neat rectangular Mycenean graves lay cut out of the solid rock, three of them still bearing an erect slab like a tombstone. Out at the southern end of the site I sat in the shadow of another ring-shaped tholos, picturing the moment when its excavators uncovered the body of a Minoan lady, maybe a princess, with her jewels around her and her mirror of polished bronze placed so that she could contemplate her own beauty for ever more. On this cool, cloudy hilltop with its grey rocks and grey stones, the Minoans seemed only a breath away.

Back in Archanes I dug out the *philakas* or guardian of the Anemospilia and got him and his key into a taxi. I wanted to have a look at the 'Cave of the Winds' up on Mount Iouchtas from close-to. 'Don't miss,' I'd been urged in the taverna last night by Zpiderman, who'd taken the trouble to lay out the story for me in his effortful English. The cave lay a 15-minute car ride off, not far below the Minoan sanctuary at the northern peak of the mountain, commanding a stunning view – east to the Dhikti Mountains, west to snow-backed Psiloritis, north across the lowland olive groves and vineyards and on over Iraklion to Dia Island lying out in the Cretan Sea. Inside the fence the site was small – three simple stone rooms side by side, each opening onto a short corridor that ran east and west. The tale, however, was both complicated and, when unravelled, marvellously intriguing – a triumph of educated guesswork.

When the Cave of the Winds was excavated in 1979, the archaeologists found the remains of three humans in the most westerly of the three chambers. One was that of a man in his thirties, the ring of iron and silver and the agate seal he wore suggesting an elevated social position, perhaps that of a priest. With him was a slightly younger woman. On top of a stone altar nearby lay the skeleton of a youth of perhaps 18, curled up in the foetal position, with a 16-inch-long bronze knife on top of him. Forensic examination suggested that he had bled to death just before being burned in a fierce fire. Outside in the corridor lay the crushed skeleton of a fourth person, a man, along with the remains of a ritual vessel.

The other two rooms contained very fine pottery – 150 vessels, in which the researchers discovered traces of fruit, grain, honey and wine. In the central chamber, on a bench opposite the door, stood a pair of feet of clay, probably the base of a wooden idol that had burned away to nothing.

The whole structure had evidently collapsed and burned around 1700 BC, the time when the first great palaces of the Minoans were all felled in a catastrophic series of earthquakes. Bearing this in mind, the runes of the

Anemospilia were read as follows. The building under the peak of Iouch-tas was some kind of temple in which various offerings were habitually made to the gods, including one personified by a wooden figure with clay feet, as in the dream of King Nebuchadnezzar. Crete was being shaken by a succession of fierce earthquakes that were destroying everything safe and secure. The jewelled man and his female companion, a priest and priestess, were engaged in a desperate ritual to placate the god who was so angrily bringing the world to ruin. Human sacrifice is not at all associated with the Minoan culture; nevertheless, that is what they were up to. They had tied up the young man on the altar, and had stabbed him by lamplight with the long bronze knife. Their acolyte, having caught the victim's blood in a ceremonial vessel, was in the act of carrying it along the corridor to place it in front of the idol in the next room when the whole building was flattened by a big tremor. This poignant stage and its actors, fixed forever in a tableau of desperation, were to lie under the earth for the next 3,700 years.

Now there was only one goal ahead, one target on which to fix the eyes and mind – the long hump of Psiloritis, dipping occasionally out of view to reappear at the next swell of the land, always closer, a white whaleback rising over 8,000 feet into the blue. Psiloritis was preying a little on my mind. After my humbling experiences with Pantelis in the Dhikti Moun-tains, was I really going to be able to take on that great lump of a mountain in the snow with my wooden stick and my leaden pack, my wonky knees, my bootsoles already losing what tread they had when I started out a fort-night ago?

In two days I crossed the shoulders of the Iraklion hinterland, and passed from the first to the second of my two 1:100,000 maps – a cause for celebration, even if the map did not seem sure, within the compass of a surprising number of miles, where it or I had actually got to. I paused only to take in a wedding feast in the big agricultural village of Profitis Ilias. It would have been hard not to; the oncoming wedding was all anyone in Profitis Ilias was thinking about, and half the village seemed to be squeezed into the taverna kitchen, the men carving hunks of lamb

The Cave of the Winds

They brought him up at dawn over the rocks,
a crag-faced priest, a woman with snakes, an acolyte
brawny and dumb. Was he a prize of war,

crying out strange prayers, trembling, tugged
on like a calf; or did he stride oiled,
prepared, a cloak of dew pearling his skin?

Earth groaned a warning. The priest muttered,
quickened step. Ruin in the temple,
leaning jambs, burst doors. The idol

lurched on cracked feet, sign of the end of things;
the greedy idol. The boy glanced in, saw
rusty stains round wooden lips. The Shaker

stretched, slabs fell. In the lamp-lit room,
curled on the altar, he heard snakes hiss.
The dumb one grinned, holding the dish low.

Bronze slipped in, out. The boy sighed,
relaxed. Out of the hill the Shaker came,
claiming heaven and earth. The god would feed.

off the bones, the women dredging steaming white mountains of rice out
of the boiler. I stopped to rest at a table outside, and had hardly sat down
before I was dished out a plate of red-hot sweet rice and tearings of lamb.
No sooner was it cleared than a plate of oily potatoes and more chunks of

lamb took its place, along with a tumbler of the groom's father's cloudy wine. A solid ring of teenaged girls formed to watch me eat and to practise their schoolroom English. You have some children? Four? Very good! How old is your son? 23! Is he married? 'No,' I said, 'he's just waiting for some nice Cretan girl.' Everyone sighed, then burst out giggling.

One cheeky lad of about ten was hanging out with the girls. His knowing little face was an irresistible blend of sweet innocence and bursting devilry, a mixture designed both to captivate and break plenty of hearts before too long. The girls were teaching me the names of common objects and writing them down in my notebook. Piato, plate. Arni, lamb. Makheri, knife. Kofteros, sharp. Young Hopeful seized the notebook and pen, wrote down a vile word and shoved it under my nose. 'Say this! Say!' he squeaked. I was not quite green enough for that. When his mother came up to see what all the shrieking was about he made a grab for the page, ripped it out, then ostentatiously swallowed it. The girls fell about. Yes – big trouble for their little sisters, I'd say, in the not too distant future.

While in Profitis Ilias I took a little walk up to the peak to have a look at the ruins of the Castle of Temenos. The stronghold was built on the mountain by Nikephoros Phokas, scourge of the Saracens in Crete, shortly after he recaptured the island for Byzantium in AD 961. He'd hoped to found a new capital city up there, safe from pirate raids. But no-one wanted to leave the fat lowlands by the sea, however insecure, for a rocky crag inland. Phokas soon left Crete for Constantinople to take on the rôle of Byzantine Emperor, and the Castle of Temenos was left on the peak as the sole monument to the fierce general's ambition.

Late on the second afternoon I came into the upland village of Ano Asites, with a great bar of cloud lying low in the valley and Psiloritis standing tall beyond, the snowy head now hidden and the eastern flanks rising formidably, filling the entire background with a rearing tsunami of pale speckled rock. You could almost hear it roaring and see it tumble forward as you looked. Down in the village under the cloud it was as calm as could be. I sat on the little terrace by the village church, took off my boots and sighed with pure pleasure. Pantelis and I were not due to meet here for another three days. Three days of inaction. I wouldn't even put foot to ground if I could help it. In three days I'd be ready to face the mountain, but not just yet. In a little while I'd go and find Manolis Piperakis, President of this local area, Mayor of Asites and – of course – a great friend of Charis Kakoulakis. 'Mr Piperakis will find you somewhere to stay, I guarantee,' Charis had said with a backward swipe of the hand as if batting troubles to the furthest boundary. 'He is a very nice man, knows everything, knows everyone, you will have no problems at all.'

Manoli and Maria Piperakis met me at their door. Once more I plunged into a linguistic hotpot of German, Greek and English smatterings, with a good helping of gesticulation. Manoli, a stonemason who had built his own living room arch and carved his own fireplace, welcomed me with great warmth. Certainly you must sleep here. It's important to get away by dawn tomorrow at the latest, and we'll give you a good breakfast before you go. What? Yes, by dawn tomorrow, of course. Yes, to start over Psiloritis. What, hasn't your friend told you? Oh, well, he phoned earlier. He's sorry, but he can't get away next weekend, so it's now or never, he says. He'll be here at six in the morning, and off you go! Feet a bit sore? Put them in this hot basin with these herbs, they'll be great in an hour. Then let's have a look at my sixteen-year-old wine, eh? Got to prepare the man for the mountain, you know!

Across the Roof of Crete
(Asites to Thronos)

'Walk about Zion, and go round about her: tell the towers thereof.
Mark ye well her bulwarks, consider her palaces … Beautiful for
situation, the joy of the whole earth, is Mount Zion…'

Psalm 48

'Ligo volta, pende lepta – a little wander, five minutes,' decreed Manoli Piperakis, slamming me into the passenger seat of his pickup at dawn. We shot round the blind corners of the village at lip-biting velocity. 'Christ …!' I heard myself muttering as I clutched the doorframe, barely awake and still in the grip of the home-made wine with which Manoli had refilled my glass so enthusiastically and so frequently last night. Cretan hospitality is a tiger, and you ride it at your peril.

'My mother and my father,' Manoli murmured, indicating the village cemetery as we roared past. I glanced over and saw tears glistening in the grooves of his face. He skidded the pickup to a stop beside a little chapel, under trees near the head of a gorge. There was something urgent in his manner, something special he wanted me to see or do.

In the silence of the chapel I could just make out a quiet bubbling of water. Manoli pushed aside the iconostasis curtain and we looked through into the apse. Water pulsed and dimpled in a little stone-lined well. 'Mothers bring children who have a problem. Children make bath in

88

this water, mother prays in the church. Problem go away.' Manoli looked at me. 'This is good water. Good to make like this before you go to Psiloritis.' He crossed himself, index and middle fingertips wet with water and joined to the tip of the thumb in the Trinity symbol of the Greek Orthodox worshipper.

I followed suit, then lit a thin brown candle. In spite of Manoli's reverence and the conducive sunrise-calm of the chapel, prayer would not come this morning. One image wiped all others from the back of my lids as soon as I closed my eyes: Psiloritis rising, the glittering snowfields, the breaking wave of pale speckled rock above its surf of low cloud.

The relationship between walkers and mountains is an ambiguous one, salted with paradox. A big mountain is a subtle beast. You live with it long before you meet it, picturing it ahead, lying in ambush. Yet you are aware at the same time that the mountain is actively stalking you, breathing on your neck until the hairs stand up. The temptation is to try to master it before you have even set eyes on it, to get it under control by pegging it down in a net of certainties: heights, distances, routes, gear, timings. You might as well try and net quicksilver.

Mountains are slippery. They change shape according to how you look at them, or think of them. If you are not careful, the shadow of a big mountain can swell and eat away at your confidence like a cancer. Quite as compelling as the desire to get its measure before tackling it is the need to scuff your boots across its slopes, to get to a place of hard scratchy reality where sweat washes away apprehension and sheer physical effort pulls you close to the bones and spirit of the mountain.

Psiloritis had taken root in my mind, and had grown there. I had read of its herby phrigana scrub, of the cores and crusts that formed it, its ledges and gorges. Friends in Crete had talked of their love for the mountain, of their fear and awe in the face of it. I heard about its stormy moods, and grew aware of the human dramas played out in peace and war in its caves and down among its skirting villages. Demons and gods stalked its hinterlands. This was Mount Ida of Cretan mythology, the place where the infant Zeus was raised in a cave by the goat goddess Amaltheia while his cannibalistic father Kronos searched the hills to find and eat the young godling. Psiloritis sheltered freedom fighters against both Venetian and Turk. At Arkadi monastery on the northern slopes, 2,000 Turkish besiegers and Cretan defenders died in November 1866 when Abbot Gabriel ordered the powder magazine to be fired. From cave mouths high on Psiloritis, British radio operators and Cretan andartes watched the Germans of Hitler's occupying forces burning the villages below the mountain. Psiloritis stood drenched in blood and history, grounded in defiance: the apex of the island, a potent symbol, its cold white head held dauntingly high against the clouds.

Back at the Piperakis house we found Pantelis Kampaxis, contorting himself aerobically on the veranda according to his early morning routine. As usual, the sight of those hawser-like muscles writhing to his scientific bends and stretches put me in deep shame of my own pale and flabby body. We sat round the table and ate a hero's breakfast: iron-hard rusks called *paximadia*, softened with a drizzle of Manoli's own olive oil and honey. Piperakis bent his arm in the strong-man sign, a clenched-fist salute to the mountaineers. 'This is food for palikares,' he grinned. 'You will be strong all day.'

Half an hour up the mountainside I put my hands on my knees and bent double, head hanging, retching as the leafy taste of Manoli's mountain tea washed back into my throat. I felt bloody. My heart was pounding halfway out of my chest. Breath gasped in flattened lungs. Sweat and suncream trickled blindingly into my eyes. Strings of saliva and snot, the result of an unsuccessful attempt to blow my nose Cretan-style straight on to the ground, hung humiliatingly from nostrils and beard as from a beaten bull in the bullring. Balanced on a rock beside me with eyes tactfully averted, Pantelis in his spandex suit of lights breathed elegantly in and out, hands on hips, not a hair out of place. 'Please to clean your nose, Christopher,' was his polite request. 'We will rest five minutes.'

The bout of distress was a wholly self-inflicted wound, easily diagnosed: too much roast lamb and red wine last night, too much breakfast this morning, and too much fast climbing while the body was still not properly awake. Nearly half the journey behind me, and still I had not yet learned these basic rules of moderation. Or more accurately: I had thoroughly learned them through uncomfortable experiences, but still lacked the self-discipline to apply them. The singing and music making round the Piperakis table, the exhibitionistic pleasure of playing my harmonica, the hum of talk and laughter had blended all too smoothly with Manoli's rich old wine, brought from its sweet smelling wooden barrel and poured with open pleasure by its author. I hadn't even tried keeping a check on the filling and refilling of my tumbler. Who in their right minds would? And this morning, who could have resisted Maria Piperakis as she spread herb-baked *paximadia* with oil and honey like some Homeric hostess?

Pantelis Kampaxis, that was who: honed Pantelis the water-drinker, the polite refuser of second helpings; steel-sprung Pantelis the stadium trainer, pounder of pavements and dedicated high priest in the temple of his own body. Pantelis had focus where I had none, which was why a thousand feet of straight-up climbing had reduced me to a jellyfish while hardly disturbing the even tenor of his breathing.

Once my eyeballs had stopped thudding, I leaned on my katsouna and admired the view back over Asites and the lowlands. Mist rose from the olive groves and vineyards. Mount Iouchtas and the distant Lasithi mountains stood flat like cardboard cut-outs of themselves, washed with muted blue, each receding wave of hills a delicate shade paler than the one in front. Near the rocks where we were resting rose a six-foot pole of faded yellow and black stripes, with a familiar tin square seized to its top. 'E4' it announced. I fetched the pole a pre-emptive admonitory whack with the katsouna. Small chance of seeing any more of those where we were headed.

Trudging on up the rocky track I gradually fell into the liberating rhythm that steals like a blessing on mountain climbers. The feet thump down regularly, one per second. Breathing heaves in the same pattern: left foot down, inhale – right foot down, exhale. The eyes cease to look hopefully upwards, and stay fixed dead ahead on the couple of yards of rock, shrub and earth unrolling downwards like a film under the sun-hat's brim. On this treadmill of the will, thoughts swirl lazily in an opiate soup. A sunken part of the mind registers with irritation the small breaks in rhythm caused by stumbles on loose stones; but most of the self rises almost without effort, a drugged spirit floating upward oblivious of blisters and aching muscles. Pleasurably adrift in a sea of blood chemicals, you only become aware of the thousands of feet you have climbed when you make a halt. '*Kalo tempo*,' Pantelis called this zen state of consciousness, 'good time.'

The Greek Mountaineering Club's Prinos hut, when we reached it nearly 3,000 feet above Asites, turned out to be a grim two-storey building with windows shuttered and barred against thieves. Not a tempting place to pass a night on the mountain. Bright metal splashes and dents made by large-calibre bullets in the steel shutters hinted at just how exciting the local wild men could make life for benighted walkers obliged to bunk down here.

Above Prinos the gradient eased. Pantelis and I made *kalo tempo* for a couple of hours, up into a bare stony wilderness and then further up to the lower slopes of Mount Koudouni. E4, according to the map, had sneaked off south and westwards; but we men of the mountains, scorning both map and waymark, were intent on sterner courses. Here was proper scrambling, hanging by fingertips and boot grips to the sheer scaly sides of Koudouni. I inched up the dark grey flank of the mountain, scraping my knuckles on its rough limestone hide. Pantelis climbed high above me, foreshortened to a pair of gouged trainer soles and two thick brown tubes of muscle encased in black shorts. Not far below the top, the handhold I was pulling down on gave way. I swung sickeningly out over a 50-foot drop. The sang-froid with which hand and boot reached for safe perches seemed to have nothing to do with me.

On the rock-strewn summit of Koudouni, Pantelis and I shook hands with the satisfaction that comes from climbing nearly 5,000 feet before midday. Peaks stood stamped on the blue sky. The upper shoulder of Psiloritis turned to the north, magnificent in a cloak of snow. Around this time tomorrow, if all went well, we would be up there in the eagle's eye of Crete. Ahead rose Skinakas, topped with the mosque-like domes of modern temples of science: the astronomical telescopes of the University of Iraklion. Down in the south-west, by contrast, the blue sky was snagged by the twin-horned peak of Mavri, the Dark One. To Mavri the Minoans came, filling the great cave of Kamares with the cream of their artistic creation in propitiation of gods beyond dreaming by contemporary minds.

⤳

Looking north from the central court of the palace at Phaistos on the Mesara Plain, a modern-day visitor can make out the mouth of the Kamares Cave as easily as could the Minoans who worshipped there 4,000 years ago. The cave is seven miles distant and some 3,500 feet above the plain, yet it shows clearly as a sizeable black smudge high in the mountain wall, with the twin peaks of Mavri curving above like the horns of a bull.

It's a hard morning's hike up from the plain, on a poorly marked track that is often obscured by clouds. But the cave, and the immense view, make the climb worthwhile. Kamares is an enormous hole. Its mouth yawns well over a hundred feet across. The roof is sixty feet high, while the cave runs back a hundred yards into the hill – roughly the dimensions of a cathedral, and with the same sense of presence in the shadows.

As with all the major Cretan archaeological sites, a local man made the first finds by chance. It was in 1890, at the start of the golden era of archaeological discovery in Crete, that a shepherd picked up some shards of old pottery in the great cave high in the southern flank of Psiloritis. When Italian archaeologists made the first scientific exploration of the cave in 1892, they unearthed pottery of a beauty and delicacy far beyond anything yet dug out of Cretan soil. Further excavations in the early 1900s, and a British dig in 1913, brought to light still finer examples of this 'Kamares ware'.

The pottery had been made in the palace workshops at Phaistos and neighbouring Agia Triada, in two distinct phases between 2000 and 1700 BC. The earlier type of pottery, probably thrown on a slow hand-turned wheel, featured red and white designs on a dark background. The later style must have been fashioned on a more sophisticated potter's wheel, perhaps foot-driven, certainly capable of much faster speeds. This type of Kamares ware is astonishingly delicate, some of it dubbed 'eggshell' in reference to its thinness, as fragile as the finest porcelain. There are wide-mouthed cups with slender handles and out-turned rims, decorated with floral bands that narrow and widen to emphasise the flowing lines of the vessel. There are spouted jugs of yellow, black and orange, and kraters for mixing wine and water whose bowls are studded with exquisite eight-petalled flowers sculpted in three dimensions. To put the sophistication of this Old Palace-era pottery in context, much of northwest Europe in 1900 BC had not yet lifted itself out of the Stone Age, while in Britain the architects of Stonehenge were still labouring to fix their crudely-cut monoliths together. Many of the best pieces of Kamares ware, retrieved whole or painstakingly reassembled, are on show in the Iraklion Archaeological Museum, where their beauty lights up the display rooms.

It turned out, after analysis of the Kamares finds, that the cave had been in continuous use as a religious centre since earliest Minoan times, around 2,500 BC: at first chiefly for burials, later for a variety of ceremonies that probably included fertility rites. Most important of all, perhaps, was the stimulus that the early Italian excavations gave to the British antiquarian Arthur Evans. Archaeologists had already pinpointed the site at Knossos, just south of Iraklion, where they suspected a great Bronze Age settlement lay buried, but it was the news of the sumptuous painted pottery found in the cave on Psiloritis that determined Evans to come to Crete in 1894 and start his enquiries into the early civilisation of the island in earnest. Six years later, having bought the suburban site outside Iraklion after the end of Turkish rule in Crete, Evans began to dig there and immediately struck gold in the form of an enormous palace. That was the epic moment of Cretan archaeology, with light flooding in on the Minoan civilisation for the first time since its collapse and descent into oblivion 3,000 years before.

~

An hour after breasting the rise of Koudouni, Pantelis and I were sitting (one of us greasy with sweat) gulping water on top of Mount Skinakas. It had been a thousand feet down and a thousand feet up again, a straight slog with no respite. But now a proper mountaineer's reward was in prospect: five long miles of gentle downward road, smoothly tarred, descending to the Nida Plain. Halfway down we heard a tinkle of bells. Round the corner of the road came scampering a flock of fluorescent red sheep. A hallucinatory moment. I blinked, wondering if the climb from Asites had been too much for me. A hundred crimson-coated sheep braked to a halt as one, took a horrified look at the two humans marching down on them, and went bouncing off the road and away uphill like a swarm of giant ladybirds. No trouble for the shepherd in charge of this flock in picking out his dramatically-dyed charges among the white screes of the mountain.

Shadows were beginning to lengthen, and the blister on my middle left toe (the big, burst one that came into intimate contact at every step with the neighbouring toenail) was making me limp painfully, by the time we got down to where the road petered out in the great green saucer of the Nida Plain. Shaped more like a lake than a saucer, in fact, this dead flat three-mile-wide grazing meadow, roughly circular, fed with mineral-rich silt and water from the mountains that surround it on all sides. In winter snow lies several feet thick on the plain; in spring, at snowmelt, the shepherding families from the mountain village of Anogia a dozen miles to the north bring their flocks up to pasture for the next six months on the rich grass of Nida. In the days before the road was tarred, the flocks would be brought up on foot, ceremonially, all on the same day. Nowadays they are jammed into the backs of battered Japanese pickups and whisked up from Anogia to the plain in half an hour.

The stone-built mitata or cheese-huts of the shepherds stand dotted round the rocky perimeter of the plain and along the road to Anogia. Each is laid out on roughly the same lines: a simple stone room with a plain sling bed, a stone-built bench seat with brushwood padding and several layers of rugs thrown over the top; a wooden table and couple of chairs; a recess for the raki and oil bottles, the plastic wine flagon, the salt and matches; a deep hollow fireplace where the big iron milk cauldron can be set to boil for cheese-making. Making cheese up in the hills alongside the grazing flocks is still a healthy part of the rural economic tradition in upland Crete, with its roots in the practical necessity of former times. Before modern transport or refrigeration, when everything had to travel on mule-back along rubbly mountain tracks, shepherds were obliged to use up their milk as quickly as they could. The cheese they continue to make in the mountains is beautiful. Some say it is best eaten warm and sweet from a wicker basket into which the shepherd's hands have just scooped it straight from the cauldron. Others prefer it matured for a few months in a cool crack in the rock. All agree it is better than the insipid stuff turned out by the ton in the lowland cheese factories.

'Terrible!' growled the old shepherd we met on the edge of the plain. Dressed in full traditional rig of black shirt, wide breeches, cracked leather knee-boots and black fringed sariki headband, he pulled up his mule and sat swaying on its A-shaped wooden saddle. 'Terrible! Going up and down to the village in their cars each day, like a set of commuters – that's what these young shepherds do these days. No time to make cheese in the mitato, like I do; no, they'd rather sell the milk off to the factories.'

'Why don't they stay up here all through the summer?' Pantelis enquired.

'Huh,' grunted the old man, 'can't put up with not having a television, I suppose. Tied to their mother's apron-strings, or their wives'. I never used to see my family for months at a time when I was a young married man. Stayed right here on Nida with my sheep, like all the other shepherds. Never did us any harm. Worst day's work they ever did, asphalting that road from Anogia.'

Grumbling on, he adjusted his sweaty sariki and glanced over my pepper-and-salt hair and sandy beard. 'Who's this? A German?'

'An Englishman,' said Pantelis. 'His father fought in Crete during the war.' This statement, not strictly accurate, had smoothed my path already with one or two fierce old men whose finest hours had been as

96

wartime members of a band of andartes or guerrilla fighters in their local mountains. They, like the younger Cretans, felt outraged at the continuing NATO bombing of Serbia. Some had given me a hard time on that subject. But their sense of an Englishman as an ally, forged once and for all when they were young impressionable men in circumstances of extreme danger and high drama, outweighed their disapproval.

My father, as a young Royal Navy lieutenant in the destroyer *HMS Hero*, had helped to put ashore Allied reinforcements in Suda Bay in May 1941 during the Battle of Crete. At some time during the heavy bomb and torpedo attacks unleashed on *Hero*, a near-miss shook her so badly that she was forced to go into dock at Alexandria for a refit. So Dad missed the desperate nights at the end of May when Royal Navy ships ran the gauntlet of air, surface and submarine attack for several successive nights in order to evacuate exhausted Allied troops from the mole at Iraklion and the beach at Chora Sfakion. It was also *Hero* that was sent on 22 May in company with another destroyer, *Decoy*, to pick King George of the Hellenes and his entourage off the beach at Ayia Roumeli and take them to safety for the remainder of the war. I had never brought out this particular nugget of personal history: Cretans are not known for their royalist sympathies.

Just now, however, the old shepherd seemed delighted. He leaned down with a creak from the wooden saddle and shook my hand. 'Your father must have been with us, the andartes. Up in the caves on Psiloritis, eh? I must have run across him.'

'No,' I said, 'he was in the Navy, a sailor.'

'Ah, a sailor? Well, what was his name?'

'John ... um, Ianni.'

'Ianni? Ianni? Let me see – yes, there was a Ianni, a radio operator who used to hide above Anogia. I didn't know he was a sailor – I thought they were all soldiers. So that was your father, was it? Good, good!' And he grasped for my hand again, shaking it as if he'd shake it right off.

'No, no,' I tried to put the old boy straight, 'that was another Ianni.'

'Don't worry,' Pantelis murmured. 'He's happy about it, whoever your father was. As long as he wasn't a Turk. They have long memories around Psiloritis – even if some of them don't work so well any more.'

⌐

When the Italians, closely followed by the Germans, invaded Greece in October 1940 in the second year of the Second World War, the Allies sat up and took notice of the big island at the southern edge of Europe. Once again Crete's geographical location – now within striking distance, by aircraft, of mainland Greece and the north-east African coast, and by naval forces of the whole of the eastern Mediterranean – would prove of vital interest to rival powers contending for mastery over this part of the world. By the spring of 1941 there were more than 30,000 Allied troops garrisoned in the island. But Germany was determined to have Crete as a forward base for attacking the Allied armies in North Africa and harassing the Royal Navy in the eastern Med.

The German airborne invasion launched at dawn on 20 May 1941 met with enormous numbers of casualties. Thousands of elite young paratroopers died before they even reached the ground, shot in their harnesses by Allied and Cretan defenders as they drifted down. The ensuing battle for Crete took 12 days and cost between 5,500 and 7,500 young lives. The Germans, like the Turks 300 years before, rolled things up from the west. There were uncounted acts of heroism, numberless miserable and desperate actions. Cretan civilians fought with great skill and ferocity alongside the troops of the British Commonwealth. When the dust settled, the Allies had been driven out. Some were evacuated by ships of the Royal Navy from Iraklion, but most were snatched to safety from the little south-western port of Chora Sfakion to which the retreating soldiers of Britain, Australia and New Zealand struggled as best they could over the high passes of the White Mountains. Over 10,000 were evacuated, amid scenes both disgraceful and honourable, during four nights of very brave activity by the Royal Navy, whose ships had to be back in Alexandria by dawn or risk being sunk by torpedo or bomb. More than 12,000 Commonwealth and 5,000 Greek troops were

Bandouvas

Bandouvas stares over ox-horn
moustaches, under black brows, a blank
peasant face stony with intransigence.

Two brandishing andartes flank him
on the sidelines; but it is the deep sunk
power of Kapetan Bandouvas we sense.

The photograph does justice to his feared
authority: high boots crossed,
slab fingers resting on the knees

that prop his rifle. Shirtsleeved judge and jury,
prisoners up before him must have guessed
his one-word sentences for blond-haired boys

dropped from the sky into such capable hands.
Scuffed toetips tell of some moonlit march.
Seated while others stand, he underlines

who calls the shots: Bandouvas the chief,
sly old wolf still hiding from the search
to find the living man among the stones.

left behind to be captured and spend the next four years as prisoners-of-war. Thousands more took to the hills, to the caves and remote sheep-folds, or entered villages to throw themselves on the mercy of the local people, who risked death if they dared to help the fugitives. Many of these abandoned soldiers were captured; the lucky ones got away by boat or by submarine.

The Cretan population, left to face the music, acted characteristically. A local resistance movement took shape even as the Battle of Crete was going on, and was continued with great resolution against the occupying forces for the remainder of the war, helped by Allied organisers and material landed in the island by caique, by submarine, by parachute and rowing boat. The Cretans soon learned that to poke the German hornet's nest usually resulted in some deadly stings. The occupiers did not scruple to burn houses, imprison and very often kill wholesale if they had been hurt and wished to make an example. On the Cretans' side, the bands of andartes or freedom fighters who formed around charismatic local leaders proved themselves on occasion every bit as ruthless as their ancestors who had resisted in turn the Romans, Byzantines, Saracens, Venetians and Turks. When Pantelis and I reached the Taverna Aravanes in the village of Thronos at the head of the Amari Valley, the day after meeting the old shepherd on the Nida plain, among the first things I saw was a photograph of Manoli Bandouvas, one of the most potent and most feared wartime kapetans or *andarte* leaders. Bandouvas and his men killed a lot of Germans. His headstrong aggression also brought a lot of death and terror by way of reprisal to the people of Crete. Sitting with one leg cocked over the other, a rifle laid across his lap, flanked by two gallant boys with machine guns, the Bandouvas of the photo looked inexorable, powerful, timeless and unknowable.

One of the worst of many incidents of German reprisal in wartime Crete took place in Anogia. If the old shepherd of Nida was the age he looked – between seventy and eighty – he would have been a young man of about twenty at the time; maybe involved in cheese-making and sheep-minding, or perhaps, as he seemed to be hinting, hiding out on the mountain in the brave and often quarrelsome brotherhood of an andarte band. Certainly he must have been away from Anogia on 15 August 1944, when several truckloads of German soldiers arrived. They had orders to shoot every male inhabitant found in or near the village, and to burn the whole place to the ground.

There had been provocation: there usually was. Anogia, a large village of independent-minded mountain people with a long history of ferocious resistance to invaders, had become one of the chief centres of guerrilla activity against the German occupying forces. The Germans knew that several well-organised andarte groups were operating from caves in the Psiloritis massif, with Anogia as their re-supply, planning and storage base. The village priest, Fr Iannis Skoulas, typified the enthusiastic resistance-mindedness of the Anogians. He obtained permission from his bishop to disguise his calling by cutting off his priestly knot of hair and bushy beard, and earned himself the nickname of the Parachute Priest by leaving the island clandestinely to qualify as a parachuting saboteur. Anogians had helped one of the resistance's most colourful Allied colleagues, Patrick Leigh Fermor, when he was based in a cave above the village. And they had been only too ready to provide food, shelter and concealment when Leigh Fermor and others embarked on their famous trek across Crete in April 1944 in the company of the German Commander of the Fortress of Crete, General Heinrich Kreipe, whom they had just ambushed and captured in one of the war's most daring and Boys-Own-Paperesque operations. The kidnap, staged at night on the road between Knossos and Archanes, was carried out with breathtaking coolness by Leigh Fermor and his fellow-officer Captain Billy Moss, dressed in hastily altered German uniforms, along with picked Cretan colleagues. They stole the General and his staff car as well, abandoned the vehicle with a note throwing all the blame on British special forces, and then hustled the wretched captive over the snowbound top of Psiloritis and sneaked him through tight German cordons before spiriting him away from the island by launch.

Opinions in Crete vary as to whether this particular game turned out eventually to be worth the candle. Certainly the propaganda value of the kidnap was enormous. Another benefit was intended to be the sowing of seeds of insecurity amongst the Germans: if this can happen to the most important officer in Crete, no German can sleep safely in his bed. Whether that effect was actually achieved is open to doubt. What is certain is that the reasonable and mild-natured man whom the conspirators removed was succeeded by the hated and feared General Friedrich-Wilhelm Müller, a former Commander in Crete whom Kreipe had himself replaced only a few weeks before his abduction. Müller was ruthless in his analysis of which villages must have assisted the resistance during the operation, and determined to make an example of as many as possible.

The fact that it took three months for reprisals to get under way suggests that Müller was looking to reap a double reward. By August 1944, two months after the D-Day landings in Normandy, it was obvious to everyone, Germans included, that the Axis powers were going to lose the war. The Germans in Crete were making plans to withdraw from most of the island and barricade themselves into an enclave in the north-west around the old Venetian city of Chania, at that time the capital of Crete. By the end of October 1944 this withdrawal had been completed, but not before General Müller had taken the opportunity to leave behind him a violent illustration of what the Germans could and would do if provoked. If the hornets were left peaceably alone in their new nest, all well and good. If not – well, take a look at the blackened ruins and blood-stained village squares of Gerakari, Kardaki, Smiles, Ano Meros, Dryes, Vryses, Saktouria, Anogia …

Down in Anogia a little two-storey museum is filled with the primitive-style wooden sculptures and naïve paintings of local artist Alkibiades Skoulas, works of art striking in their directness and uncluttered clarity of vision. One of the paintings shows graphically what happened in Anogia on 15 August 1944. Green-clad German mountain troops roam among burning houses; guard dogs snarl and tear the corpses of executed partisans; villagers wait in line to be gunned down.

The painting is a record of complete destruction. Today scarcely one house in Anogia predates 1944. Only the village church survived the burning. Altogether forty-five men were shot dead, thirty of them villagers of Anogia. Nowadays a large marble plaque stands in the village square, incised with the words of General Müller's proclamation of 13 August 1944. It lists various resistance activities carried out by the villagers, and ends: 'Whereas General Kreipe's kidnappers passed through Anogia and stopped here, we order it to be levelled with the ground and every male

Anogian found in the village or within one kilometre of it to be executed.' The plaque is an object of pride, against which elderly Anogians with a claim to having been an andarte will consent to be photographed. But it also stands as a piece of defiance, a warning to any potential oppressor, who has only to look around at the present-day thriving village that has sprung from the smoking ruins of 1944 to know how futile such an act of repression would be. You can't keep good Anogians down, it says, so don't even think of trying.

This kind of robust self-confidence underpinned the decision of the Anogians to accept the German artist Karen Raeck when she came to live in Anogia in the early 1980s. Raeck wanted to make a tangible expression of sorrow, admiration and reconciliation on behalf of her countrymen. Up on the Nida Plain she created a work of art she named *Andartis*, a huge recumbent sculpture of a freedom fighter a hundred feet long and thirty broad, using large rough rocks from the surrounding slopes. The Nida shepherds gave their seal of approval for what she was trying to do by helping her shift the boulders into place. There might still be a few anti-German growlers and grumblers in Anogia, but most of the younger generation seemed to agree it was time to move on.

∽

Pantelis and I bid the old shepherd goodbye and walked across the cropped green sward of Nida, tired out but unwilling to come to an anchor. Great flocks of sheep moved slowly across the plain. A male and a female shepherd approached each other from opposite sides of the plateau, dwarfed by the backdrop of Psiloritis 3,000 feet overhead, taking their time, yet drawn magnetically to the same midway spot. A couple of minutes' chat; then the two cloaked figures separated, each beginning the long geometrical journey to where the other had come from.

We climbed the slopes above the plain until we could look down on Karen Raeck's *Andartis*. It lay sprawled across one corner of Nida, a freedom fighter with legs bent ready to spring, one bouldery arm pointing at full stretch into the hills, the other weighed down by a tear-drop shape that might have been a battle shield, the furled wing of an angel, or simply a tear for the pity of war. Interpretation seemed redundant up here in the buttery evening light.

The big modern taverna at the northern edge of the plain stood empty at this early season of the year. The woman in charge was packing up for the night when we walked in, but she delayed her departure for Anogia long enough to dish up lamb chops and salad, the Cretan staple. Entrusted with the keys, we found a couple of beds in a bare little room upstairs and enough cold water for a splash.

We were sitting in the restaurant when a creak of boots in the doorway announced a luxuriantly moustached shepherd, one of Anogia's numerous Stavrakakis clan, attracted from his mitato on the far side of the plain by the taverna lights. Pantelis brewed thick sweet Greek coffee. The shepherd eyed the plate of cheese pies that the woman had left for us. 'Go ahead,' said Pantelis. Stavrakakis picked up a pie in blunt fingers blackened with wool grease and posted it whole under his moustache. Then another. His gooseberry green eyes flickered here and there, never resting on one object for more than a second or two, a little unfocused as if more used to staring into distances. The cheese pies continued to vanish, one by one, under the fringe of the drooping moustache.

Sheep rustling was the biggest problem on Psiloritis, the shepherd told us between mouthfuls. There were more sheep and goats on the hills than ever before, thanks to European Community subsidies, and some people evidently saw that as an opportunity to put together their own flock out of what they could steal from their neighbours. They came across the mountain at night, from somewhere south. It was easy enough to take twenty sheep out of a flock, if you knew what you were doing. Couple of good quiet dogs, a moonless night. Personally, Stavrakakis wouldn't be surprised if men from Zoniana were behind it. There had been bad blood for generations between Anogia and Zoniana, a kind of rolling feud down the years. Violence? The shepherd grinned. Yes, I myself have been shot at. But I have a good gun back in the mitato, and a couple of nasty dogs. Also some brothers. We haven't lost a sheep yet. They'd better not try.

'Do you know my brother-in-law, George Aphordakos?' Pantelis asked. Aphordakos the runner? Oh yes, everyone knew Aphordakos. Hadn't he stayed sixty days by himself on the plain, training, running up and down the mountains like a champion? That was a man who could run from Nida to Anogia and back in one hour: a man, in fact, who could catch blackbirds in his hands. So legends start.

It was a beautiful evening on Nida, with the music of sheep bells filling the plain. Behind the taverna the central bulk of Psiloritis loomed, sending an inky shadow creeping out to swallow the hills in the east, one by one. Pantelis yawned and stretched, looking across to the still sunlit tip of Skinakas. 'Christopher ... I think I will go for a little run, to relax the muscles. Just up Skinakas and back – just one-two hours. We must sleep well tonight.'

Off ran the iron man. We had climbed and descended some 8,000 feet today, and covered perhaps 15 miles in eight hours on the hoof, but Pantelis was still on fire. I watched him spring away down the road, as light and energetic as a whippet. Then I slumped over a beer, sleepily watching the shadow of Psiloritis snuff out the foothills and scribbling ideas for poems.

In the night I woke from a tangled dream. Slow quiet breathing came from the bed where Pantelis slept, head pillowed on hand, goatee beard making a neat dark circle on his moonlit face. I slipped out of bed and crept downstairs to stand at the taverna door and scour out my head. Sheep bells tinkled from the unseen slopes. The moon gave out a frosty light. Psiloritis rose like a white whale against a black starry sky, with a spume of cloud streaming eastward from the crest. Leaning shivering against a pillar, I experienced a sense of release. The mountain that had weighed on my mind all these months was lifting clear; no longer a hydra-headed monster eating away at the imagination, but simply a presence of great beauty, a calm shape anchored to the plain, faintly radiating snow light into the night.

A superb blue morning dawned over the mountains, and we were way up high to greet it. The wind had swung round and was pushing hard from the north-east, exhilaratingly cold. Nida lay spread a thousand feet below, its flocks drifting like lemon yellow clouds in the sunlight. None of this was registering with me at the moment, however, as I snotted and sweated through the pain barrier. The only realities half an hour into the climb were the dusty trainers of Pantelis ticking ahead like metronomes on a level with my face, the clatter of loose rocks squirming underfoot, and the urgent need to reach the zen plateau of *kalo tempo*.

Another hour, another thousand feet of climb. Heart, blood, lungs and thoughts had slowed to a smooth interdependent flow. It came as a shock to find the first snow crunching under my boots at 6,000 ft. I looked up. Snow in a blinding white sheet, rising steeply to meet a dark blue sky. Pantelis a couple of hundred yards ahead, putting on sunshades against the glare. Next thing, my nose was in the snow and my boot soles in the air.

I had walked on mountain snow before, but never on snow like this. The Inuit would have a word for it: snow up to five feet deep in the hollows and perhaps a foot thick on the mountainside as a whole, snow with a coarse crystalline crust over a slippery, icy subcutaneous layer. Nine footsteps out of ten sank an inch into the crust and were held there; the tenth would break through and skid backwards on the skating pan below. Bit of a problem. Eventually, after a couple of knee-jerking falls, I worked it out. Kick in the boot toes with each step, jab the katsouna down, and lever upwards. An effective way to make progress, but a tiring one against the strengthening mountain wind. Soon a whole chorus of leg muscles was backing the solos of complaint from my toes, already blistered from their prolonged pounding on Cretan limestone rubble. Why hadn't I nipped up and down a few Welsh mountains for practice last winter, my body wanted to know. How could I have been so casual in my preparation for this adventure? Didn't I understand it was hurting?

'Christopher!'

Pantelis's shout from above broke the surface of this sea of self-absorption. The wind had snatched off his black and yellow cap and thrown it playfully down the mountainside. As the cap came spinning past I let go of the katsouna and launched myself sideways in a goalkeeper's slide across the snow. The recklessness of the dive amazed me. Whoever it was, skidding down the slope on his back, it certainly was not the timorous fellow who had quavered his way into the Valley of the Dead a fortnight before.

Only those who share my lifelong inability to make bat, racquet or hand connect with an oncoming ball will understand the pure thrill of pleasure I got when I came to a stop a few seconds later, opened my eyes and found the cap wrapped round my skinned fingers. 'Manchester United!' was Pantelis's one-liner as he resettled his headgear and handed me my stick.

Now there was time to look around as the climb went steadily on. The snow surface was not the unblemished white sheet I had taken it to be at first. The storm winds of winter and the warm sunshine of early spring had powdered it with rock dust and smeared it with meltwater mud. Under overhanging ledges, and at the rim of corries such as the one we were now inching up, the snow had been sculpted into quiffs and waves by wind flow. Where it had melted, pale mauve mountain crocuses were already pushing up among the spiky cushions of *astivitha*. Cretan sage grew there, too, its whitish flowers set among pale furry leaves. 'With these we make mountain tea,' said Pantelis, 'mix with honey, make you strong for walking and not to be sick.' Somewhere up here the herb-seekers find dictamos or dittany, the famous cure-all marjoram plant endemic to Crete which the islanders used to say was eaten by wounded deer and wild aegagros to expel the hunter's arrows and heal the wounds. Dictamos keeps out the cold, cures headaches and fevers, increases a man's stamina on the hill and in the marriage bed. You should not trust the dried stuff they sell in cellophane packets down in the town markets, Pantelis had advised me. Better to use dictamos freshly picked from the mountains. But there was none to be seen around the snowbound slopes we were traversing.

Like the Page in Good King Wenceslas, I followed the footprints of Pantelis over the brow of the corrie. An ice-cold wind gave me a shove tough enough to make me stagger. Beyond an intervening valley the high, ship-like prow of Psiloritis came into view at last, a magnificent white nape rising steeply to the summit. I put my head down, pushed my frozen hands into my pockets and plodded up the final rise. Up at the top at 8,058 feet, a giant cairn of roughly fitted stones poked out of deep snow. Pantelis and I embraced, yelling with delight, the highest men in Crete. Tiny icicles clung in the cropped hair of Pantelis's moustache, and wind tears streamed down his cheeks. A huge grin split his goatee. The wind sang out of a royal blue sky. It was a wild and overwhelming moment.

After the celebrations, the hundred-mile view: a compass-wide panorama to all points of Crete. I planted my stick in the snow and turned round and round while the wind tore at jacket and trousers, feeling the island revolve like a propeller around the hub of Psiloritis. Back in the east, cut out of blue lead, the jagged spines of mountains I had crossed: Lasithi, Dhikti and Thripti, Iouchtas and Skinakas standing proud and closer. To the north the sugar-lump sprawl of Rethymnon at the edge of the Cretan Sea. Down in the south the glinting strips of a thousand greenhouses reflecting the sun from the Mesara Plain, the twin humps of the Paximadia islands lying in Timbaki Bay. Fifty miles off on the southwestern sea horizon, the hunched cloud-like form of Ghavdos Island. And dominating the view to the west, straddled sternly across my future, the craggy white peaks of Lefka Ori, the White Mountains, bunched formidably together like turrets rising from a dour castle wall. A breathtaking panorama. I felt the breath actually leave my body in a rushing gasp. I took off my hat and faced the White Mountains bareheaded, an instinctive gesture, part propitiation, part admiration.

'Come on,' called Pantelis, 'let's eat.' We crouched against the cairn in the lee of the stones where the wind could not get at us, nibbling goat cheese and olives, speculating on the identity of villages seen far below. Something was puzzling me. Where was Timios Stavros, the chapel of the Holy Cross that was said to sit like a jewel on the crown of Psiloritis? I had been treasuring in anticipation the moment of pushing open the door of the little summit church to see the flagstones on which Nikos Kazantzakis had surrendered his virginity in the clutches of an Irish girl, under the furious gaze of Christ from the iconostasis.

'Here it is,' said Pantelis, puzzled by my question. He slapped the rough stones of the cairn. 'Timios Stavros, the Holy Cross.' I stared at the stone pile. It did not look like a building, let alone a church.

'But – how can I get inside? Where's the door?'

Pantelis grinned and poked a finger into the snow where we were sitting. 'You'd better start digging, Christopher. The door is down there, two metres.' Light dawned. The winter's snows had completely buried the little church, and the spring melt had so far done no more than expose the topmost stones of the structure. We had been eating our picnic on the chapel roof.

It was too goddamn cold and windy to stay on the roof of Timios Stavros, let alone that of Crete, for more than a couple of minutes. The wind literally blasted us off the peak and down the west face of the summit, chasing us down the contours until the angle of the slope shut its howling away. We descended a long, slippery valley where I had to learn the heel-and-toe technique all over again, in reverse this time. Drive in the heel, stamping out a little step in the snow; balance on the katsouna; a step down with the other foot. Repeat. Repeat. And repeat. Ever been tobogganing on your arse with your back hair in the snow? It's a curious sensation. After a couple of hundred feet of acceleration I fetched up against Pantelis. Once I'd reasserted sphincter control, vast amusement all round. Back to the old one-step. Could this careless snow-stamper and involuntary glissader of the slopes be the old anxious me? It seemed so – for the present, at least.

At last the snow lay behind us, and we descended through woods of maple and prinos trees, following a zigzag shepherds' road. The shepherds of Psiloritis had spoken for centuries of a wild cat, a fourokattos or 'fierce cat', glimpsed by them from time to time in these mountains. Nonsense, scoffed the scientific community; Crete could never support such an animal. Sheer old wives' tales. Then in 1996, only three years before I walked through Crete, an Italian research team found a *fourokattos* in their trap cage one morning – five and a half kilos of spitting, snarling, tawny-coated ferocity, according to their understandably awestruck report – not far from the mountain slope that Pantelis and I were descending. The Cretan mountains, evidently, still held signs and wonders.

Down at last in the village of Kouroutes, eight hours after setting off from the Nida plain ('Kalo tempo, poli kalo,' said Pantelis), we sat on the terrace of a kafenion and drank *hypovrichio*, 'submarines' – a lump of icing-sugary vanilla paste apiece, sunk in a glass of water and clinging to a spoon whose handle rose like a periscope above the surface. Deadly sweet, and deadly good. We chatted and dozed above the empty, sunny street. A taxi staggered by eventually, and we headed off up the valley to Thronos and the Taverna Aravanes.

Here Pantelis and I said goodbye. In prospect for me, a week at least of lotus eating in the Amari Valley, the Shangri-La of Crete. For the tireless aegagros Pantelis, a bus ride back to Iraklion, 'and a little training at the stadium tonight, Christopher. Only one-two hours – and of course a little run also. I am quite tired, so maybe just up Mount Iouchtas and back. Or maybe *little* further ...'

Lotus Land: Amari interlude

'I am like a green olive tree in the house of God.'

Psalm 52

Each morning I am woken around five o'clock by the braying of the old donkey that lives on the hillside below my bedroom window. The donkey belongs to Nikephoros, the white-bearded healer of Thronos, and eats its own weight of God knows what, all day, every day. It never utters except to roar in the dawn, a signal for the village cocks to tune up and make with their one-word salutation. They in turn set off the dogs, who have been observing – more or less – their nightly three-hour truce in the barking war they have been waging with the dogs of Kalogeros and Vistagi for the past 4,000 years.

I groan, swear, turn over and thump the hard pillow to make a barrier between me and the dawn choristers outside. In the rooms along the balcony each side of mine I can hear Patricia Clark and David and Wanda Root doing much the same thing. Snoring resumes on both flanks. But it's no good as far as I am concerned – now the bloody finches have noticed the first flush of morning light touching the horn-shaped apex of the mountain of Katsonissi that stands opposite the village, and they, too, begin to chip their four eggs in. More groaning, more swearing, and I slop out of bed and go out on the balcony, scratching and yawning like a tramp.

Of course it's beautiful out there. The light is between pearl and peach, the air cool but holding the promise of a warm spring day. There's a hint of wild sage and a breath of wood-smoke. Beyond the balcony, the picnic terrace and miniature vineyard of the Taverna Aravanes give way to an enormous prospect. The whole of the eastern side of the Amari Valley is in view, sloping away south-eastwards for the best part of ten miles. To my right, across the donkey's hillside and a steep little valley beyond, rise Katsonissi and other hills nameless to me, the dawn light broadening across their slopes, their ridges marching down towards the bulgy and ill-shaped lump of 3,300-ft Mount Samitos which hunches like an island to split the smooth south-eastward flow of Amari. It's all green and pleasant enough over there, as it is far below along the valley floor where well-watered meadows and pale green cornfields lie among the trees. But my gaze, as always, is drawn towards the east, high above the villages scattered on the slopes there, over the tight white huddles of Kalogeros and Vistagi, above Platania and Fourfouras beyond them, way up over the zigzag dirt roads and the dark forests of pine and prinos, up 6,000 feet by bare rock canyons and the skirt of the snowline to the twin-horned head of Psiloritis, still velvet dark with its back to the sunrise, outlined against the last of the night's stars.

This view never ceases to do the trick and bring a smile to my face, no matter how sore my fingertips from yesterday evening's laouto-playing or how many tumblers of Lambros Papoutsakis's glutinous home-made wine showed their bottoms to the moon after midnight. I drink a glass of water, fetch pen and notebook from my bedside, and stealthily ease the balcony chair to the table. Nikephoros's donkey has stowed its gab for the day, but Maria Papoutsakis is already at work below, picking tender vine leaves to make *dolmades* with soft, crisp plucking noises. There's a sputter of two-stroke across the valley as another early riser scooters along the back road through Kalogeros. While my fellow guests and carousers continue their interrupted slumbers, I sit in the soft blue light of early morning and make up some doggerel – or donkerel – in tribute to Thronos's long-lived and long-eared public alarm clock. Apart from eating a few more of the oranges I bought from the fruit-man, this – unbelievably, deliciously – is all I have to do today.

Donkey dawn

Before the sun begins to glow
On valley fields or mountain
    snow.
Before the day is truly born,
Thronos awakes to donkey dawn.

I lie cocooned inside the deep
Contentment of a sweet night's
    sleep,
Until I hear that first forlorn
Unearthly sound of donkey
    dawn.

How pleasant it would be to
    glide
To morning's shore on songbirds'
    tide,
Instead of being rudely torn
Out of my dreams at donkey
    dawn.

I jerk awake when first I hear
That opening, long-drawn,
    brassy blare –
No Cretan driver honks his horn
More stridently than donkey
    dawn.

A breathless silence then ensues,
As at receipt of awful news;
A second's hush, that soon will
    spawn
The real row of donkey dawn.

Is that a smoker being sick

With laboured heavings hoarse
    and thick,
Or is it timber being sawn
Inside my head at donkey dawn?

It sounds as if the village pump
Is being worked with wheeze and
    bump,
Slowly, with handles old and
    worn,
By sadist fiends at donkey
    dawn.

And now the roosters raise their
    din,
And all the village dogs join in;
The last vestige of peace is shorn
From hill and grove at donkey
    dawn.

I will not stand it one day more
My bags are packed and at the
    door;
By all the curses I have sworn,
I will be quit of donkey dawn.

Yet when I wake in Bristol
    town,
Where noisy cars roar up and
    down,
And students vomit on my lawn
–
I'll miss the sound of donkey
    dawn.

During the Second World War, Allied officers working clandestinely with the Cretan resistance nicknamed the Amari Valley 'Lotus Land'. They came to love its abundance of the earth's good things and the open-handedness of its villagers. Nothing has changed. Amari is green, Amari is fruitful. Amari has mineral-laden streams off the mountains to water its gardens and carpets of wild flowers to clothe its roadsides. Floating in its wide cradle of mountains 2,000 feet above the noisy, nervy, tourism-orientated world of the coast cities, Amari tends its gardens, its olives and vines, its figs and walnuts. Individual sounds travel far between the echo-boards of the mountains, muted and softened by distance: the orange-seller groaning *'Portokali-aaaaaa!'* through his cab-mounted speaker, a radio sending a whining snake of a lyra tune out through the almond blossom, the dogs of Vistagi issuing their eternal sore-throated warnings. Everyone takes time, everyone gives you a nod and a word: Nikos the joker with the walnut tree in his yard, George the taverna laouto-player and conversationalist, Andonis the church cantor and lyrical lyra-player, and the three men named Kostas whose path I cross most days: Kostas Pervolia the green-handed gardener, Kostas Raki the village raki-maker, and Kosti Lyra the goat-eyed musician from neighbouring Kalogeros, a master of the lyra who can make those three strings scream, sing and sob as if an angel were behind them – or maybe a devil.

Now between the horns of Psiloritis the high saddle of the mountain darkens. A fingernail of silver pokes up behind the snowy ridge, turning to gold even as I squint at it. The cocks of Thronos redouble their monologue. The crescent becomes a spinning silver-golden ball, unbearably bright, appearing to dance between the bull-horns a second before lifting off to float free into the china-blue sky. Minoans must have watched this daily crowning of the great mountain from their peak sanctuaries across the valley, Dorians from the city state of Syvritos on the flat hilltop behind Thronos, Byzantines and Venetians from the square by the little frescoed church, Turkish janissaries and German soldiers on reprisal duties from the smoking ruins of Amari villages. Now it is this middle-aged *tourista* who raises his eyes from his half-finished verses to the dazzle and drama over Psiloritis.

∽

'Good morning, Lord Christopher,' says Maria Papoutsakis, coming into the big taverna room with her arms full of greenery.

'Good day, Lady Maria,' I riposte, 'and how are you today?'

'Well, thank you, Lord Christopher. And you also?'

'Yes, very well, thank you, Lady Maria.'

We are still at the stage, Maria and I, of addressing each other with some formality – she, because her manners are excellent; I, not to be outdone in the offering of courtesies, but also because I like the sound of this stately *'Kyrie Christophere'* and *'Kyria Maria'*. It lends a graceful gallantry to our exchanges that transcends the generally mundane subject matter:

'Lady Maria, do you perchance have a plug for the basin in my room, if you please?'

'Why, certainly, Lord Christopher, here is one.'

'Thank you so very much, Lady Maria.'

'Lord Christopher, please – the pleasure is entirely mine. Thank *you*.'

Patricia Clark, my Canadian next-room neighbour, is mightily tickled by this, and insists on addressing me at all times as 'Lord Christopher'. Patricia is a classicist from Victoria University, Alberta, a fluent speaker of Greek, over in Crete for three months to continue her long-term study of the islanders' traditional methods of healing – by herbs, by folk remedies and by magic. She says that all three of these branches of practical medicine are alive and thriving in the Amari Valley. Last year, researching traditional use of plants in the Amari, Patricia stumbled across a handwritten book of medical recipes and treatments, spells, charms and magical rituals, compiled in 1930 by a local healer – an incomparable treasure. Now she sits with Maria Papoutsakis, sorting vine leaves into various sizes on the big taverna table. They mean to make a big pile of *dolmades* for today's memorial ceremony for an old man of Thronos who died six months ago. It is proper to remember the dead at certain intervals after their passing.

I take a cup of coffee and sit out on the steps barefoot in the early sunshine. Since crossing Psiloritis yesterday and descending into Lotus Land I have scarcely given my feet a thought. Now I make a damage inspection, the first in the hundred miles since Kritsa. Left foot, existing damage: little toenail now turned from blue to grey, and hanging loose (it falls off as I touch it, and another, pink and perfect, is revealed in its place). Blister inside front heel still there; blister on ball of foot now flattened. The whole ball and heel a rather disgusting, rubbery yellow hide, pitted with black holes – none of this, strangely, to be seen on the other foot. Blister on outside of big toe still there, and has been joined by a little friend. New stuff: big burst blister on 4th toe, rubbing against and partly underneath 3rd toe. Large and bloody abrasion blister on outside of ball of big toe. Curious blemish like a double wart on top of root of big toe. Hmmm. Right foot, rather better. Existing damage: Achilles abrasion almost healed, rub marks ditto, blisters now burst and healing nicely. New stuff: small blister on outside of big toe. And something very new and sensitive to the touch coming up on the outside. Watch this space. As for olfactory forensics: Stinkerismo Grandissimo would about cover it. Memo: why do feet smell of goat? Why not of bread, or dog, or roses? I hobble back upstairs. I intend to spend at least a week here in the Amari, maybe more, to give the snow that now covers the White Mountains the maximum possible chance to melt away and leave me clear passage. In the meantime, bed calls, and those oranges. Maybe another poem, too.

Towards evening I sit on my balcony and stare out at Psiloritis. There is no escaping the dominance of the horned mountain, rearing like a breaking wave over Amari. A saddle of snow lies between the peaks. High over Vistagi the snow has part-melted into a curious figure like that of a football-headed man with no arms, a long torso ending in two straddling white legs. It reminds me of Karen Raeck's *Andartis* flattened in mid-stride to the Nida plain, or of one of those giant figures cut into the chalk downs of southern England. With bees buzzing murmurously among the hillside herbs below and the sun striking warm through the valley, I contemplate the mountain and my own fears and falterings.

In the evening Patricia returns from the old man's memorial with a dish of *koliva*. It's the traditional titbit at such ceremonies – sugary, fragrant, seeded with little silvery sweeties. Greeks have been making it since long before the birth of Christ. Patricia tells us how it's done, from what she has herself been told by the village women. Boil wheat with the leaves of an orange tree. Sieve it. Spread it out and roll it on lemon leaves. Add

The high man

The high man straddles over Vistagi:
not that they see him there, though their
dogs bark warnings day and night.
Theirs is a spring view, a window looking
west into the bowl of Amari, green
watered valley, terraced and tended, where
grass lies lush, bees investigate new sage.
Behind their back the high man walks
winter, behind the bald nape of the gorge,
above road scar and tree line.

Yesterday I learned that ground
for dear life, breathlessly hammering
each step with my heel, descending the snowfields
and rock slides where the high man hid.
Cold fingers stroked my neck, cold breath
told of his closeness as I passed,
seeing only snow hard packed into a gully.

Watching him now through vine and olive leaves,
deep in the drowsy valley, I see
the high man small and shrinking. The sun
will have his head, Salome-like;
trunk and legs will run through the forest;
all the springs in Vistagi will sing
the high man's prophecy of summer.

I know him now. Away from green pastures,
up every rocky track, the high man
walks winter and waits for me.

to the broth: orange leaves, sesame, cinnamon, chickpea flour, sugar, salt, walnuts, raisins, pomegranate seeds, nuts, parsley. Incense it well with a church censer. Take a tray of it in procession to church, covered with sugar and decorations, along with raki, oil and a lit candle. Thus one eases the path of the soul.

We eat with Maria Papoutsakis, dolmades, salad and damp new cheese. Maria's husband Lambros, owner of the Taverna Aravanes and my friend from past visits, will be back tomorrow night from Rethymnon, she says. George the laouto-player joins us, and the wine goes round. George speaks no English, but he drops a slice of apple in his wine 'to sweeten the talk'. Soon the laouto case is brought out and the big round-backed instrument is lifted from its red velvet nest. 'Play us a tune,' gestures George to me. As the senior, in truth the only proper musician present, he's offering the stranger a pleasant courtesy. I can't spurn his civility, but neither can I really play. George hands over a thin strip of plastic, doubled to form a narrow and flexible vee. It's the *pena* or laouto pick. I've never handled one before – Dimitri's laouto in the Taverna o Pitopoulis back in Prina had come complete with a familiar plastic guitar plectrum. The pena used always to be a vulture feather, George remarks. When he started out playing laouto, a vulture pena would cost 50 drachmas and last one session in the hands of a good vigorous musician. Now, if you can by chance and good luck get hold of one, it costs 5,000 drachmas and lasts a hundred sessions. Why? 'Because vultures are getting harder to kill!'

Everyone in the place laughs, then falls silent and looks on expectantly. I grasp the awkward shape of the laouto to my chest and try to remember a mandola tune – any tune. In the end I strike up an old Incredible String Band number, Schaeffer's Jig, a tune I can be absolutely certain no-one here will know, and one I can doubly guarantee will never have been forced from this or any other laouto. Four bars in, George's fingers gently imprison my pena hand. No, Christophere. Like this. He repositions the business end of the pena between my thumb and the tips of my index and middle fingers, with the two loose ends of the vee trailing out along the back of my hand. It feels bloody odd, but I soldier on as drops of pure sweat of embarrassment plop down on the fretboard. Two times round the circuit and I fall silent. D minus for execution. Yet applause is forthcoming, and smiles of genuine pleasure. With a nicotine-rich laugh, George refills my glass. A for effort, it seems. The stranger has put his handful of potatoes, however small and green they may be, into the communal pot, and is entitled to share the stew.

Now George begins a series of mantinades, sung with great force and emotion, aimed at appropriate targets among the company. Maria Papoutsakis sits nearby, joining in the verses. These traditional expressions of love, aphorism or pithy commentary may be well known to those present, but here they are sung as if freshly minted and passionately felt. With the laouto in his hands George is transported beyond intensity. His eyes glitter and burn as they flick between the fretboard and the face of his victim, his nostrils dilate, his voice shakes as if in the hands of some vindictive god. It's as if he has reached a state of electrical charge. If Kostas Raki, sitting alongside, were to reach out and touch him as he sings, it would be no surprise to see blue flashes arcing between the two of them.

Patricia, who has been asking George to clarify certain recondite plant lore for her, becomes the recipient of a mantinade.

> *'Do not cry, you worrier,*
> *For the world is not being destroyed –*
> *With the plants of the earth*
> *All suffering is healed.'*

She grins at the lightness and aptness of the sally, while I, struggling with the colloquial terms and elongated sounds of the sung words, smile and clap uncomprehendingly with the only other two monoglots in the taverna. David and Wanda Root, the middle-aged American couple whose room adjoins mine, are from upstate New York, very gentle in manner, very much in love with each other and with Cretan 'graciousness'. George fixes his gaze on Wanda's pretty round face, jerks his head, fills his lungs.

Has Patricia mischievously whispered a translation of Wanda's surname in the singer's ear?

> *'At the full of the moon*
> *Other trees don't take root –*
> *Only the tree of love,*
> *Which always extends its root.'*

People grin to themselves. Everything is cool. Here in the quiet pastures of the Amari Valley these two compatriots of Beelzebub Beel have faced no breath of criticism, no challenge from anyone. The Taverna Aravanes maintains an old-fashioned dedication to food and drink, talk and song. Its big bar TV is hardly ever on, so no serpent from Kosovo has yet sneaked into our green Eden or disturbed our fair dreams with toxic little stabs of bad news from beyond the boundaries of Lotus Land.

Lambros Papoutsakis returns to Thronos for the weekend from Rethymnon, where he has been spending the week working in a bank and dreaming of the day when he will no longer have to wear a suit and tie, but can retire to the hills and tend his taverna and his vines full-time. On sight of me he tilts his head on one side and throws his arms wide, sighing, his face breaking out into a turned-down grin. 'Christophere, Christophere, Christophere ...' He enfolds me, then lightly slaps my cheek. 'Why have you not been in Kriti for so long? You are very bad to forget your friends.'

For several years I have made the Taverna Aravanes my base of operations whenever I'm in Crete. Lambros is not just a friend, but a mentor. He has taken me far into the secret places of Amari, far into the village celebrations, the singing walks and moonlight expeditions that are the breath of life to him. On a mountain precipice he will pose in proper palikare style, curly shepherd's stick held out at full extent of his right arm as if he would gather rocks, plants and birds under his protective wing. Wandering the byways of Amari he has Psiloritis constantly in view, and speaks of the mountain as a friend, occasionally as a god. Once, climbing on Psiloritis to find the grave of an old man killed in a wartime German

The hollow stone

The hollow stone, black-eyed, skull-like,
lay among prinos, partisan trees
of great Psiloritis, pressed to the mountain
by weight of brute winds, but apt to stab.

Lambros, you struck the pose heroic,
bold on a craggy perch, arms flung
wide to embrace outspread Amari.

Fire in the veins: fire in Vrises,
Meronas, Gerakari. Old men's bones
charred in reprisal; eyes in the prinos,
burning, recording – these you venerate,
honey-hearted Lambros.

The hollow stone
winked a dark eye: whisper or thought
lodged in the inner ear, timeless.

Many-celled womb, a wild bees' comb
clung in this cranium scoured by the centuries'
gales to pruned strength, nurturing sweetness;

sign from the mountain, great Psiloritis.

revenge raid, we picked up a hollow stone and discovered a tiny honey-comb clinging by a thread inside. Lambros brought it home and built it into the wall of the Taverna Aravanes, part keepsake, part talisman.

Lambros is the Green Man of Thronos, a cornucopia of newly shelled almonds and freshly cut artichokes forever in his hands, a glass of wine always filling on the table, trailing mantinades and prayers in his wake. In him palikare and aegagros seem perfectly in balance. Every time I have to tear myself away from Thronos and descend to the drab lowlands of life once more, it is with a head refilled by Lambros with a new stock of songs and dances, of wayside herbs and mountain flowers. Bags of *dicta-mos*, little plastic bottles of raki and jars of sweet, smoky honey from his hives rustle and chink together in my suitcase, to be spilled out on the table at home with a burst of scents that bring the warm and sunlit essence of Amari to my dark northern kitchen.

❧

May Day dawns cloudless and hot. 'First of May, big picnic,' announces Lambros. All Thronos is packing its baskets and heading for the hills. 'Thou hast made us to drink the wine of astonishment,' forecasts the Psalmist, and he's absolutely spot on.

Up at Lambros's vineyard we decorate his ancient pickup truck – rickety, rattling and all but brakeless – with nosegays. David and Wanda, Patricia and I fill our hat bands and buttonholes with flowers. We clamber into the truck and go jolting up dirt roads towards the woodland party. Among the oak trees several dozen people from the villages round about have gathered around a big square fire fenced in with spits. Meat hangs roasting in chunks and chops, racks of ribs and whole sides of lamb. There is a great dripping and spitting of fat, and a wonderful smell. Tables hold bread, cheese, bowls of salad, bowls of seasoning, wine and raki in plastic bottles. Blue wood-smoke veils the view out west over the trees to the distant snowy peaks of the White Mountains.

A bowl of choice titbits of offal is passed around; then the main feast begins. It takes me a few minutes to work out the etiquette of proffering and accepting food and drink in this setting. I follow Lambros's example and arm myself with a wooden spit of meat chunks, a knife, a little tower of small plastic cups and a 2-litre bottle of wine. The trick is to juggle these without letting anything slip. You slice off a sliver of meat and place it directly in the mouth of friend or stranger, then follow it up by handing over half a cup of wine. Now you accept in turn your share of this rustic Eucharist, which mixes the savour of roast meat, the sherry-like richness of village wine and the pungent bite of raki. Empty cups reclaimed, both of you nod and smile your thanks and move on. After ten or so encounters of this sort I feel myself pretty well browsed and sluiced; by the time I have completed the courtesies with forty fellow-picnickers, and notice that a whole new rake of roast pork is being pulled from the spit and more wine and raki bottles are being fetched from the parked pickups, I start to wonder whether I am going to prove quite man enough for the First of May.

A young fellow in a red T-shirt comes up. 'Hello!' I say brightly in my best party Greek. 'Happy May Day! My name is Christopheros – what's yours?' The man scowls and glares. 'Beel Cleenton – bombas!' is his reply. 'Beel is fucker ... fuck Beel!'

This isn't good. I imagine he has been provoked by the quiet upstate New York accents of David and Wanda, who are sitting modestly with friends from Thronos on the edge of the party. I try to muster a reply, but the angry boy stomps off. Later that day I learn that a missile from a NATO plane has cut a bus in half on the Pristina-Podujevo road in Kosovo, killing sixty civilians. The boy must have been listening on his car radio as he drove to the picnic, arriving hot with fury. Now his friend comes up, a dark-browed youth in a black shirt who has had a cup or two. 'Yermanika? Amerika?' he asks aggressively, and leans into me with clenched fists. I find myself suddenly fluent in Greek. Oh no, I am English, I love Crete, I hate war, war is terrible, Crete is beautiful, my father was an andarte here in the war (may God and Dad forgive me), Lambros is my friend, do you know him?

He does know Lambros, and subsides. We rally. There is a general gathering in a clearing under the oaks. Musical instruments are brought from the trucks. Andonis the Thronos church cantor, a calm man with a classic Greek profile, sits with his back against a tree and carefully tunes

123

a lyra across his knee. A keening tune gets under way as the laoutos join in. A line of dancers forms, stepping sideways and back among the trees, dancing the siganos, the dance of friendship and unity. Lambros is in his element, twirling with his daughters, a flower behind his ear.

One dance follows another. The sun begins to decline towards the White Mountains, and there is a drifting away of revellers. Empty plastic bottles, lamb and chicken bones, tatters of silver foil and shreds of ejected tomato skin lie everywhere. Patricia, David and Wanda have disappeared. By six o'clock a hard core of a dozen dancers and players remains under the trees. Goat-eyed Kosti from Kalogeros has abandoned his mandolin and has taken over the lyra. The summery flow of Andonis's playing gives way to thunder and lightning. In Kosti's hands the lyra whimpers and screams. He jags the bow into the strings, rapping the body of the instrument with sharp smacks, now burying his face in his chest, now tossing it up to the sky, teeth bared in a rapturous grin. The dancers shake themselves into new life. The daughters of Lambros have gone home, but he dances on, sometimes alone, sometimes with an arm around the shoulders of friends, far out on some ecstatic sea. I sit among the musicians, anaesthetised by meat and wine, entranced in the whistling of the lyra and the ringing, percussive thud of the laoutos.

The youth in the black shirt looks up from his laouto and beckons me to his side with a jerk of his head. Lambros catches sight of me as he reels by. He bends his face close to mine, trying to articulate. Black-shirt lets his instrument fall and clamps our three heads together, an acknowledgement of a moment's drunken and euphoric bond. Someone very close pulls out a large black pistol and lets off three shots into the treetops. Lambros vents a wild laugh, and shouts out words no-one can catch.

At dusk the survivors come to a decision to move on elsewhere. I get into Lambros's old pickup with some trepidation. After several unsuccessful attempts to fit the key into the ignition slot, Lambros looks round as if in a dream and enquires wonderingly, 'Where is this?' He has certainly had a lot to drink, like all of us, but his state is more that of a man transported onto another plane entirely. Our progress down the dirt roads

The First of May

The older man starts. An axe blade smile
slashes his face, a fixed grin of absence.
Across his knee the lyra shivers, pours
a distillation: braided flowers, oil,
sizzle of sheep fat, Homeric sounds
and sights – clouded wine, the singing air
under the oaks, a blue strip of hills
holding the ring, a low shimmer of fire.

Now Kosti takes it. Tips his goat head
to the sky, thrashes the bow. Blood
and drink tilt the trees. A pistol cracks.
Hands tug my hair, friend or foe
plunging me to the dance. The voice of Lambros
burrows in my ear: 'Now we are mad ...'

contains more excitement than I think I want to deal with. Soon we pull up outside a house where the lyra and laouto players are gathering, all with a second wind on them. Here I leave Lambros in the arms of Orpheus and set out on foot. Thronos, when I reach it, lies quiet under a brilliant starry sky, its spell broken only by a single barking dog. That's until some of the picnic revellers turn up at midnight, bringing the spirit of Pan with them. They forage for food and play till dawn.

The Psalmist, of course, is all for locking the doors on such wild fellows: 'They return at evening; they make a noise like a dog, and go round about the city. Behold, they belch out with their mouth ... Let them wander up and down for meat, and grudge if they be not satisfied.'

Lambros turns up at the taverna the following evening, very subdued, and sits drinking lemonade and groaning gently to himself. He is not the only one.

⌣

A quiet day of spring in Lotus Land, with a blue heat haze on the mountains and the songbirds warbling in the middle of the day. Lambros is back in Rethymnon, sweating out the working week in his bank. I sit and yawn on my balcony. 'Thou crownest the year with thy goodness, and thy paths drop fatness,' sings the Psalmist. 'They drop upon the pastures of the wilderness: and the little hills rejoice on every side. The pastures are clothed with flocks; the valleys also are covered over with corn; they shout for joy, they also sing.'

I have certainly dropped some fatness on the paths and the pastures of Crete over these past three weeks. My feet are healing nicely, and only sheer bloody indolence is keeping me on this balcony. I stick a bottle of water and a couple of oranges in the day pack and take myself off for a good walk along the roads of the upper Amari. All is very quiet and empty in the hot sun. Green-backed lizards flick off the road, where they have been stretched out soaking up the heat through their pale bellies. One or two have taken up permanent residence where the tyres of passing cars have smoothed them into the tarmac.

I am looking for the church of Agios Ioannis Theologos, St John the Evangelist, a place with reputedly good 14th-century frescoes which has eluded me on a couple of occasions in the past. Now I find it tucked down below a bank in the olive groves a mile outside Kalogeros. The frescoes are black with age, but a strikingly serene Christ Pantokrator occupies the bema, the rounded sanctuary beyond the iconostasis. Scaffolding poles, planks and bags of concrete, piled against the church wall, hint at a restoration at some future date – perhaps very far in the future. It is one of the scandals of Crete that so many of the island's 800-odd frescoed churches are left to the ministrations of snails and damp. Yet over-restored church frescoes (there's more than a hint of that about the Panagia Kera in Kritsa) can lose something precious under the revisionism of the rehab

126

brush – the tidemarks of history in cuts and slashes struck into the paintings by religious bigots, the graffiti of naughty village boys, and in the very tracks of the original painter's brush the sense of connection across six or seven centuries with that medieval artist's own particular person.

Across the valley in Meronas I walk into the church of the Panagia, All-Holy Mary, to find the restorers actually at work. Perched on planks, paintbrushes in hand, they are picking out details of the paintings in the nave roof. These frescoes are stunning, especially a Crucifixion with a horribly agonised Christ, a calm Good Thief already sporting a halo, and a grotesque buffoon of an unrepentant thief with a bulbous Cyrano nose, clearly – if the face is the mirror of the soul – already on his way to the nastiest corner of Hell. Propped up carefully against the scaffolding I find the 14th-century icon of a sorrowful Virgin. The Panagia guards the church, and must not be removed; so the villagers have warned the restorers. The Virgin's long, long face and nose, her little pouting red mouth, are illuminated by a pair of deep, mournful eyes. These have been scored across several times by a knife-point – 'Turk' is the one-word explanation of the restorers. But the Virgin continues to gaze reproachfully out from her glassed-in captivity, commanding the gaze of the onlooker even through her scars.

On the road to Gerakari I pass over a bridge above a spring deep in a dell. A stone washing slab lies beside the spring, and I fantasise about scrambling down there and taking off my sweaty shirt just for the pleasure of washing it in that cold, clear water and pounding it on that cool stone slab under the fig trees. To point up the painful gulf between fantasy and reality, E4 signs begin to show their black and yellow faces at the roadside. Casting doubt and caution to the wind, I decide to follow them and the map to Gerakari. Big mistake. Between them they lead me a long way up a thorny hillside, and abandon me just where the thorns are thickest. Bastards. Back to the road with scratches on arms, legs and face.

The houses of Gerakari, square and plain in modern concrete, offer mute witness to the terrors of war in which a village can literally be blown to smithereens and wiped from the map. Gerakari possesses a still more direct and emotive testimony to its tragedy of 1944 – a war memorial composed of a giant marble sculpture of a woman in classical dress, in the act of chiselling the names of the murdered villagers into the face of a monolithic square column. As General Friedrich-Wilhelm Müller served Anogia in the aftermath of the partisan capture of the German Commander of Crete, General Kreipe, so he dealt with the villages under the Kedros range of the western Amari which were deemed to have offered help to the andartes on the run with their valuable prisoner. The village war memorials record the progress of the burnings and executions through the valley from 22 to 30 August 1944. That first day, 22 August, the German soldiers hit six villages between Gerakari and Ano Meros. The memorial in Kardaki lists nineteen names from four neighbouring villages. The big marble monument on the edge of Vrises honours thirty people, including five surnamed Korounakis and four of both the Thountedakis and Troullinos families. As for Gerakari, forty-two were killed, including nine of the Kokkonas family and six of the Koutelidakis. Altogether the Occupation forces destroyed nine villages and shot 164 people. This was just in the one week-long operation in Amari.

꠵

From a cave high on Psiloritis, George Psychoundakis watched the unfolding nightmare, as he recorded in *The Cretan Runner*:

'I stayed there two or three days before leaving, watching the Kedros villages burning ceaselessly on the other side of the deep valley. Every now and then we could hear the sound of explosions. The Germans went there in the small hours on the twenty-second of August and the burning went on for an entire week ... First they emptied every single house, transporting all the loot to Retimo, then they set fire to them, and finally, to complete the ruin, they piled dynamite into every remaining corner, and blew them sky high. The village schools met the same fate, also the churches and the wells, and at Ano Meros they even blew up the cemetery.

They shot all the men they could find ... They launched this cruel campaign to terrorise the entire island, and to show us all that the Germans in Crete still had the power to destroy and overthrow, as barbarously as ever, all that still remained standing.'

⤚

Back in Thronos in the cool of the evening I find that Patricia's son Doug has turned up for a few days' lotus-eating. He's a tough young guy, pleasant-mannered, with a close-cut beard and dark sapphire-blue eyes. Doug's the head warden of a polar bear reserve at Churchill, way up in the Arctic Circle on the western side of Hudson Bay, and a few days in the warmth and greenery, the vivid colours of Amari represent to him an unbelievable treat.

In the warm still night, under the stars of Amari, we receive his talk of snow and ice, of polar bears and Inuit laughing contests and frozen hunting expeditions, as we might the yarns of a Baffin Bay harpooner or a foretop-man returned from the Great Southern Ocean. There's some sighing and head-shaking around the table. Doug is treated with deep respect, his talk with just a shade of dignified reserve. Local pride is ever so slightly on its mettle, perhaps. Thronos is full of wonders, too, even though there are no polar bears.

⤚

Now my time in Lotus Land begins to trickle out fast. The weekend comes round again, bringing Lambros with it. He has great plans for an expedition to Psiloritis. In the end it is Doug and I who set forth with him on Saturday morning, the feast of Agios Ioannis Theologos. First port of call is the village church – not the ancient, frescoed church of the Panagia, but the more modern church dedicated to St John the Evangelist. It is a pleasure to hear Andonis – last seen playing lyra in the Dionysian atmosphere of the May Day picnic – in his alter ego as cantor, intoning responses and passages from scripture in a deep, dramatic voice. Two priests officiate – Papa Dimitris, the long-term incumbent of Thronos who looks with his cloud-like beard exactly like a saint from a fresco, and a visiting priest from Amari. Every now and then one or the other pops out of one of the two doorways in the iconostasis for a few seconds of chanting before retiring into the bema again, a double act irresistibly reminiscent of those wooden weather dolls of the 1950s, one with a brolly and mackintosh, the other in sunglasses and short sleeves, who would foretell the weather in the twin doorways of their snug little house on the mantelpiece of every maiden aunt worth her salt.

The Amari priest delivers a rousing sermon carefully tailored to his rural flock – God is present in our vineyards, our fields, our olive groves; He enters our houses invisibly, like television, whether we will it or not. When it comes to Communion, he holds the platter of bread just out of my reach, and gently enquires, 'Katholico?' 'Ne,' I reply, remembering at the last moment that Greek 'yes' is English 'no'. 'Kalo, kalo,' he says softly, 'good, good.'

Though the Orthodox and Roman Catholic churches have been divided for a thousand years, there's an understanding between them. The Orthodox faith as practised in Crete seems to have a humanity and a directness of personal contact that mainland Greeks have sometimes felt to be lacking in their church. Maybe it's the fact that recent reform in that mainland church has placed a high premium on further education among its priests, while Crete has generally maintained a more low-key approach; maybe it has to do with the vigour of many Cretan priests, their willing-ness to dance and play music, and the very active rôle that Greek Ortho-dox priests in the island played in the front line of resistance against both Turks and Germans. Whatever the reasons, in an age of falling church attendance, especially among young people, observance of the faith still stands pretty central to up-country Cretan village life.

Priests, above all, are expected to be approachable. When on another occasion I went across the valley with Lambros to the saint's day feast in his native village of Petrohori, there was a general murmur of recognition and of pleasure as two priests got up and danced together – a murmur that affirmed the pivotal position, in the past and the present at all events, of the priest in the life of the countryside.

Priests dancing at Petrohori

In the covered place by the church
two priests dance. The plump one with the
smile trails a grey hem.
His brother-in-Christ, pigtailed, pale and precise,
has neatly tucked up his black skirts.

Petrohori feasts. I raise my glass to kiss the
snowy cheeks of great Psiloritis, guardian mountain,
as Lambros unchained has kissed mine.

Smack clay dust from your shoe soles, you
young Petrohori farmers. Tense whining of
lyra, foxy glances of the players
judge your moment faultlessly,
the skyward flight of feet and spirit

beyond what your fathers aspire to, or your shuffling
grandfathers, sappy old men crooking
arthritic knees, swinging polished boots in the dance.

Linking old ones and young step the well-matched
brothers, soberly, black shoes held to the dust.
Some day, following tradition, wolves may
again menace the flock. Then priestly soles
will rouse the clay once more round Petrohori.

Outside the church after the service, Manolis the kafenion owner dispenses shots of raki. We break off chunks of *artos*, sweet spicy bread, from a loaf whose shiny crust has been indented with the sign of the cross. Manolis beckons us into his lair for more of the same. It's two o'clock by the time we are bouncing and groaning in Lambros's rattletrap pickup along the dirt road from Vistagi and up across the lower slopes of Psiloritis. The afternoon is very windy, with rags of cloud streaming through the valley. We stop frequently on the way up, to talk to shepherds we meet *en route* and to give the pickup a respite from its climbing duties. It has no hand-brake, but a stone wedged under each bald tyre does the job well enough. We pull up at a little chapel with a bell hanging in the tree outside to pay our respects at the railed tomb of Myron Litinas. 'Shot and burned by the Germans, 3.9.1943, aged 77,' reads the inscription. Behind in the rock lies the cheese cave of the Litinas family. In the front part of the cave a hearth has been built, complete with a circular hollow of stones to support the cauldron of boiling milk. The cool cleft behind has been fitted with rows of wooden shelves for storing the cheeses that the Litinas men will make this summer. Plastic bottles of oil and wine stand wedged into cracks along with boxes of matches, cooking utensils and a tinfoil screw of salt. 'They will be here making cheese tomorrow,' offers Lambros, 'or maybe the next day, or the next.'

Back at the pickup Lambros revs the engine while Doug and I kick the chock-stones from under the hopeless old tyres. Then it's on and up to the mitato at the end of the road under the saddle of Psiloritis. Here are stone benches and a stone table, plenty of shade from the sun under prinos and asfendos trees, and a deep fire pit in which Doug does the guy thing with dried prinos branches and matches till a wobbly blue heat spiral begins to ascend and blow away on the mountain wind. Lambros produces a blue bowl full of pork chunks marinated in his special relish and spears them on sharp spits of prinos. And I fetch salt, artichokes, bread, cutlery, wine, oranges, broad beans and olives out of the flatbed of the pickup.

We eat, slowly and deliberately, for at least a couple of hours, chatting desultorily, enjoying the wind and sun and the mind-bending view. The

Shepherd

Forehead polished egg-brown by sun, fingers
stiffened to thick roots: he dumped himself
in ancient jeans down by our fire, then hauled
hard on each knee – crack! – to bend his legs.

Thick dusty spectacles shaded eyes bleared
by seventy years' looking for sheep in sunlight
merciless on white slopes of Psiloritis.

He cocked his head up like a dog, sniffing
the talk, assessing, weighing us well.

A high old voice, rapid, parched, loosened
by raki downed in a gulp, like stones in a dry
streambed set chattering by spring rain; and loud
from lack of use through lone days, lonely nights.

Moustached like a sage, bristled like astivitha,
so he sat, head back, peering through wrinkles,
shooting out words, cracking his knees, and watched
his flocks, his dogs, and us, missing nothing.

wind turns cold, gusting strongly enough to upend our glasses and scatter bread crusts and artichoke leaves across the ground. Clouds thicken in the west, but only to 5,000 feet; above this the jagged white teeth of the snow-covered White Mountains rise against a cobalt sky, as do the horns of Psiloritis at our backs. Below the cloud belt the Amari Valley lies in a thick opaque light, ridges and bluffs looming mistily far below as if underwater.

An old shepherd turns up and sits with us, sluicing Lambros's raki down his throat. It seems many days since he has heard a human voice. Behind dusty spectacles his eyes, taking us in glance by glance, are faded blue. He speaks in a cracked voice, his words tumbling over each other in his eagerness to be heard. You could take him for a distracted, even a disassociated man. But I have a feeling he doesn't miss much.

Towards nightfall a couple of teenage lads arrive in a pickup to do the milking. The shepherd clambers away up the mountainside and drives the sheep down in a bleating, bell-clonking flock. The boys chivvy and beat them into the pen behind the mitato. Then they take up station, one each side of the exit gap. From either gatepost hangs a loop of rope padded with a sausage of cloth like a horse's collar. Into these milking straps the boys stoop until the padding lies across their chests. Then they let themselves swing forward, suspended in the padded straps from the anchoring pillars. The simplicity and ingenuity of the arrangement makes itself clear as the milking begins. As the sheep, driven from the rear by the old shepherd, made for the exit, the front runners find themselves grabbed two by two by the lads and deftly hauled round until their udders are neatly positioned over a pair of big milk buckets on the ground. Swinging forward in their straps, the boys empty each udder in a dozen squirts and release the owner to go prancing and leaping to freedom. We time them at it – 15 seconds per sheep, and about 400 in the flock. Milking the whole bunch is under an hour's work for the two boys. God knows how long it would take, and how much backache, if the lads had to bend and straighten continually to catch, subdue, position and milk each one of those 400 sheep.

While milking continues we wander off across the slopes of Psiloritis. Lambros pulls us up on the brink of a fearful slot in the limestone that opens grey lips ten feet wide. 'Sink hole,' he says, 'throw in a stone, Christopher.' We hear it bounce once, twice and three times, then no more. Glancing in, I see a black rock funnel chuting away into darkness. A gleam of old snow lies at the bottom. A hundred feet down? Two hundred? I begin to realise that Iannis Pantatosakis had meant what he said about the dangers of sink holes in the White Mountains, covered in a treacherous crust of thin snow through which the lightest walker might plunge. Once at the bottom of a funnel like that, you could shout all year long and never be heard.

Back at the mitato we are invited within. A roaring fire of thorns burns on the hearth. The cheese-hut is a single plain room with light bulbs drooping from a wire that crosses the low ceiling. There's a bed by the fire, a table, a store cupboard. The bare necessities. Here Iannis the shepherd has to stay all summer, from the arrival of the sheep after snowmelt to their departure for the valley before next snowfall. Why? asks Lambros. The shepherd gives a one-word reply. Lambros translates: 'Sheep stealers.'

At last it's time to go. We stumble out onto the mountain in a windy, cloudy night. Jolting down the dirt road with its endless hairpin bends, the pickup develops a squeak that Lambros has never heard before – 'new music,' he calls it – to go with the symphony of rattles, clunks, splutters, shudders and ominous grinding noises that are its normal accompaniment. Second gear fails halfway down the mountain. Then the headlights falter and go out. It is ten o'clock at night when we eructate to a stop outside the Taverna Aravanes where Maria and Patricia have been chewing their nails on the doorstep since sundown, convinced we have gone over some precipice and are lying in pieces at the bottom, never to be found again.

My last day of Amari idling. Patricia, Doug and I take a box of fancy biscuits and pay a call on Nikephoros, the healer of Thronos, and his wife Aretousa. Nikephoros in his mid-seventies cuts a splendid figure, in looks rather like one of those heraldic Chinese dragons, with a halo of white hair and a splendid white beard swept back from a face seamed with wrinkles and tanned by all weathers. A pair of extremely sharp eyes looks out between a snub nose and bushy dark eyebrows. His hands are those of an artist, delicate and expressive, the fingers tapering to a leaf-shaped point.

Nikephoros is a maker of lyras, like his father and grandfather before him, seeking out asfendos trees on the slopes of Psiloritis to make the boat-shaped bellies of the instruments. He shows us a couple of his lyras, each with a bull of Minos poker-worked into the back. The instruments shine with a dull lustre that enhances every knot and whorl of the asfendos wood. It's produced by applying *enopnevma me to propoli*, a mixture of raki-like spirit and the sealant that bees use to construct their waxy combs. So says Nikephoros, pouring a dark red drop onto the lyra from a tiny bottle. It is just one of dozens of cures, potions and healing plants that he brings out for our instruction over the next couple of hours, as Patricia questions and takes notes. The healer is a bit of a showman, too, delighting his audience by striking sparks from a piece of granite with a flint and setting fire to a chunk of *mikita*, tinder fungus.

Aretousa, a humorous woman with eyes as bright as her husband's, brings a basket of herb-baked *paximadia* and dishes of soft *misithra* cheese, beans and olives. The wine and raki bottles are uncorked. Nikephoros drinks his raki from a tiny screw-top jar. Soon the lyra is tuned and played, and the table in the long, narrow front room becomes littered with flower stems, crushed leaves, bunches of herbs, olive stones, shot glasses, lyra bows and bits of scribbled-on paper. The air smells of warm bread, strong spirits, beeswax, herbs and burnt mikita, a savour that we carry round with us for the rest of the day.

Late that evening Lambros takes off for Rethymnon, leaving the imprint of his stubbly cheeks on mine. I feel quite bereft for a few minutes. Then the Kalogeros lyra-player Kosti turns up at the taverna. Free from all constraints, he lets himself rip. Mantinades pour out of his mouth. Long extracts from Kornaros's epic 17th-century heroic poem *Erotokritos* are accompanied by the wildest of clashing, scurrying, screeching lyra. Kosti's head pushes forward, his mouth extended into an abstracted 'O', eyes alternately shut, rolled ecstatically ceiling-wards, or fixed unnervingly on and at the same time beyond each of his listeners in turn. It's a breathtaking display of unbridled musical ferocity. Kosti plays until the dawn is almost on us, and only goes away when the wine runs out.

Next morning I say goodbye to Patricia and Doug, and eat my final breakfast in Lotus Land – another palikare-style one of dictamos tea and special spicy paximadia – under Maria's tearful gaze. I give her a big hug and kiss. 'Farewell, Lady Maria. I am so grateful for all your kindnesses.'

'No, no, Lord Christopher, the pleasure has been entirely ours. May you go to the good! May God travel with you!'

I take a quick look at the map, trying to make a rough calculation of distances. I reckon I have covered some 170 miles, give or take. Maybe 130 to go? 150? In my current state of mind and body, after a fortnight of lazy hedonism, I really couldn't give a monkey's. I shoulder the pack (how awkward and heavy that feels after two weeks' respite!), give the figwood katsouna a preparatory twirl, and walk out of Thronos. At the top of the rise under Katsonissi I take a last look back at the little huddle of white houses at the head of the valley. A couple of strides and it all passes out of view.

To Sfakia: A Rock and
a Hard Place
(Thronos to Chora Sfakion)

'He shall give his angels charge over thee, to keep thee in all thy ways.
They shall bear thee up in their hands, lest thou dash thy foot against
a stone.'

Psalm 91

The pack was beginning to oppress me in a serious way. Somehow the weight seemed wrong. I stopped by a bulbous old olive tree on the outskirts of Gerakari and took it off to investigate. My big plastic water bottle had mysteriously gained a twin. I unscrewed the top of the newcomer and sniffed. Ah! Kostas Raki's finest and best – two litres thereof. Maria Papoutsakis must have quietly slipped it in among my possessions this morning, a not-so-little memento of Thronos. I re-shouldered the pack and went on. Weight, shmeight.

Along the mountain road beyond Gerakari I stopped at a little kafenion for a glass of lemonade. The owner, a big slow-moving woman, was shelling broad beans into a bowl at a table outside. Are you from Germany? Where are you going? Where have you come from? The heavy local accent and clipped-off phrases struck oddly on my ear after my fortnight among friends and English-speakers. I was going to have to get used once more to being the stranger, the odd man out.

'You look very hot and sweaty,' remarked the woman with concern. I was feeling hot and sweaty, yes. The bloody pack, raki and all, was bowing me down. The old sins of commission – too much of Lambros's wine last night; too much of everything nice but naughty, in fact, during the interval in Thronos. Well, I was heading away from all that now. I kicked a rush-bottomed chair to the table, sat down and helped my hostess finish her bean shelling. My reward: a good double handful of the long green pods, for later consumption with a lick of salt and a snifter of Château Kostas.

The mountain road led upwards for mile upon mile. In spring a walker tastes the Cretan countryside – the abundant birdsong, the scent and colours of the wild flowers, the tingle of clear spring water on the palate, the rippling grasses – with a pleasure that has vanished from the over-farmed and polluted land of Britain. In the rocky uplands between the hills of Mavro Soros and Mouri I caught and hugged to myself the kind of ecstasy which inspired all those generations of folk songs that began: 'As I roved out one May morning, to view the valleys and the sweet flowers of spring ...'

At the western edge of the plateau the road dipped in a series of loops and contortions into the lower country around the big regional town of Spili. Paved alleyways and mazy lanes took me down under the huge cliff that rises at the back of the town, depositing me at last in the main square by a gorgeous Venetian fountain – nineteen lion heads all in a row, their snarling mouths gushing water from the hills. The Green Hotel proved to have a room, and a balcony for drying my clothes. The taverna I chose for my evening meal had a problem with its wood-burning grill, but Mr Stratidakis the owner, nothing daunted, fetched his wife's hair dryer and soon had the fire blown to a roaring heat.

A French couple paused by my table. A very, very fit-looking couple. The man eyed my plate of chops and spuds, my jug of village wine. Are you walking? Really? This is not good food for a walker! It is necessary to train properly. He patted his washboard stomach, lightly, with satisfaction. I was 60, three years ago, and to celebrate the fact I walked all the way from Le Puy-en-Velay to Santiago de Compostella. 1,500 kilometres – 50 days! All on foot! All alone! Thus one should celebrate an anniversary, and not, if you will permit the observation ... Well, at all events, goodnight to you! 'And *bonne nuit* to you, *salaud*,' I allowed myself to mutter through a mouthful of hair-dried and delicious chips. Back at the Green Hotel I discovered that the French couple were my next-room neighbours, and enthusiastic snorers to boot. Well, bollocks. Just a nip of Château Kostas, why not ...?

I woke to find sunlight on my face. Eleven o'clock in the morning. I was lying on the bed fully clothed. Realisations: (a) Lotus-eating is as tiring as walking. (b) Raki is a tricky friend, and a subtle enemy. I left the rest of the bottle in the room, and hoped the next guest would investigate and appreciate the master craftsmanship of Kostas Raki.

By the fountain I met an old man with a rubber-tipped and knotty stick. 'Orea katsouna,' I ventured. With snippets of Greek, and a lot of pantomime, we compared stick notes. So yours is from Kritsa, eh? Well, well! May I have a look? Yes, this is really fine. Who gave it you? Aphordakos? Can't say I've heard the name – unless it's the same family as that young runner in the mountains. It is? Well, isn't that good? Mine is only a *European* stick, I'm sorry to say. Hardly a stick at all, in the real sense of the word. But this one of yours – now this is a proper Cretan katsouna! I wish I had one. Wouldn't care to swap, I suppose? No – well, I'll just have to get someone to go to Kritsa and fetch me one, won't I? Here it is, sir. Look after it! Goodbye, now!

The youth of Spili's secondary school, outside the gates on their lunch break, were not so courteous. In fact they ran me out of town with some shouts and a shower of small playground pebbles. News from Kosovo? Or just smalltownitis?

E4 came sidling up outside Spili, tugging at my elbow like an ingratiating lover. Oh please, forgive me for my lies and my deceptions. I promise I'll be good, really I will. Let's just go down this nice flowery lane, why don't we, and see if we can't start over. We kept company together, gingerly, for a few miles, not exactly in close communication but not entirely estranged, through Agia Pelagia and Koxare, Angouseliana and Paleol-outra. Here I discovered with a thrill that I had just walked into the final side of the map. Now, where to stay tonight ... E4 seemed to offer nothing for the next seven or eight miles. How about Kanevos, an hour's walk to the west? As if miffed that my attention had strayed, even for a second, E4 upped and offed, disappearing into the ether without a backwards glance. Decision made, then.

Rent Rooms Iliomanolis stood at the head of a most beautiful gorge, Kotsifou. I took a stroll down there from Kanevos in the late afternoon under towering and spectacular rock walls. Their opposing curves, if the canyon should happen to have snapped shut, would have fitted as neatly together as a pair of spoons. A clonking of goat bells drew my binoculars to a cave hundreds of feet above, where a couple of goats were noncha-lantly browsing. Swifts on passage north from Africa darted about on their evening feeding flight. Above in the blue sky a gryphon vulture wheeled, no doubt waiting (bleached bones on the gorge floor suggested) for one of the goats in the cave to try for a juicy tuft of greenery just that bit too far out of reach. And a dove with pink-grey plumage and a barred tail sat shrilling out a trembling, silvery call on a prinos branch near the top of the cliffs. There were many prinos around the gorge, hunched into clefts, crouching on the skyline, clinging to cracks with contorted roots. I realised how much I had come to admire these mountain trees with their eternal strength, their subtle adaptation to circumstances and their capac-ity to put up with and even thrive in the harshest of conditions. If ever there was a tree to symbolise the Cretans, it would have to be the prinos.

In the early evening a young boy with a katsouna big and curly enough to put mine to shame drove a great herd of goats down from the pastures at the rim of the Kotsifou Gorge to be milked, their neck bells making a beautiful melodious ringing – the music of the Cretan highlands. My host Manolis and his wife sat at their kitchen table, stripping the spiked leaves from a vast mound of artichokes. It took them a good couple of hours. I offered my help, but only succeeded in jabbing my fingers so badly that I got blood all over the artichokes and my one clean shirt.

Prinos

Prinos, prickly oak, I have admired you
guardsman tall on a skyline, challenging
all weathers; have seen you hold goats high
in sinewy hands; have met you crouched in gullies,
dwarfed by wind, your fingers dug into
cracks, a grim survivor; and have passed
your whitened corpse, toppled to a grave
among dry boulders in a gorge bed.

Tamarisk shades the beach; asfendos sings,
lyra-shaped; men sit under
plane trees, nibbling olives. Iron-hard
prinos, you make an everlasting crook
for goatherds; indomitable, you take your stand
on mountains, shoulder hardship, and endure.

Next day I made north-west at a good lick across the narrow western waist of Crete, leaving the Libyan Sea and the south coast behind me as I set off, and topping a rise within a mile or so to see the Cretan Sea ahead in the Gulf of Amirou on the north coast of the island. Over the grey wall of the Lefka Ori foothills to the west peered the conical crests of the highest White Mountains, still blanketed with snow. They seemed to have marched very close all of a sudden. Whether I was going to be able to make a direct crossing through the High Desert heartland of the White Mountains, or whether I would be obliged to take the south coast route with its great gorges, was not really up to me. In the end it would be the Clerk of the Weather who would give the high-level route the thumbs up or down. Having seen the sink holes on Psiloritis, I knew the heights of

Lefka Ori would be impassable under any kind of snow blanket. I needed sun, lots of hot summery sunshine in the next few days, to melt that late-lying snow. It was just a question of wait and see.

In the month since I set off from Kato Zakros the thistles, poppies and mulleins had all flowered. The roadsides were a madman's palette of splashed and spattered colours. Down in the tree-hung village of Moundros I got directions from a kafenion owner. See that old kalderimi? Down there, past that black and yellow sign, says *epsilon tessera* on it – that'll tell you you're on the right track. Then you just kind of follow the valley to the north, due north, all the way to Argyroupolis – OK?

Hello again, E4. Side by side my inconstant lover and I descended the cobbled pathway and made our way through olive groves and stands of cypress into a gorge. Marked on the map? No. The track rose to run through the ruins of a deserted village high on the hillside, then passed a nice bold yellow and black waymark on a boulder and continued its climb as a well-engineered, carefully walled kalderimi. An hour later and 500 feet higher, I pulled out the compass. I was heading due south. Too disillusioned even to curse, I retraced my steps back into the ruined village.

Just beyond, the track split into two identical paths. One up, one down, neither going north. The map, for what it was worth, showed the path dipping shortly to cross a river. I ventured fifteen minutes along the down track. No signs, no river. Back to the fork. Up the left track for fifteen minutes. No signs, no river, and no northward trend. Not a sound among the trees. I stopped, and could feel my heart beating heavy with rage. Back to Moundros and face a three-hour slog along the tarmac, with Argyroupolis, the City of Silver, a mile away at most? A month ago, confronting the same kind of obstacle at Vori, I'd lacked the confidence to grit my teeth and go for it. Now, with 200 miles and plenty of bumps and bruises, inside and out, under my belt, I was absolutely damned if I was going to go all the way back to Moundros with my tail between my legs. I carried on down the up track, and smacked the first E4 sign I came to so hard I thought I'd cracked my katsouna. It was just as well I hadn't, because round the corner, just where the track swung decisively north

Those dogs

Those dogs that writhe black lips back
from traps of teeth, that burst their chains,
that prowl the tracks thirsty for blood
the colour of mine, that leap fences,

scale walls, gallop the hills
with lolling tongues dripping; dogs
that snarl and hackle, tear and rip;
dogs adrift, abroad, aflame

with killing lust: I know those dogs,
have nurtured them, have laid them on
my trail myself. Every hour,
on every path, I will outface them.

and sloped towards a water splash, an oil-barrel dog kennel blocked the way.

I had given myself many a talking-to about my Cretan dog phobia. Generally speaking, I love dogs, and they get along pretty well with me. That was the funny thing. No matter how much I tried to reason with myself, no matter how many times I told myself that no packs of rabid hounds roamed the Cretan mountains, somewhere in my psychological backpack the worry drum beat on. By this stage of the walk I'd got a fairly clear idea that it had nothing to do with reason; that the dogs were just four-legged, fang-baring middle-aged anxieties, running loose in my head but nowhere else. I wrote a poem to expel them and to chide my inner coward, and tried to think of something else.

Cretan dogs – the real ones – have a bloody time of it. I'd grown used to seeing them roped short to iron stakes in the full sun, or chained like this one into a makeshift kennel, usually an old metal barrel guaranteed to become an oven in summer, a fridge in winter. Sympathy for their plight as a race, however, wasn't going to get me past this particular cur. I took a firm grip of the katsouna and sidled up level with the barrel. Diogenes looked to be fast asleep. He also looked to be a cross between an Alsatian and a timber wolf – the dog, in fact, of my pre-adventure nightmares. I took a step forward. Like a flash he was out and at the end of his rattling chain, snarling like a lion and doing that terrifying dog thing that involves twisting blue-black lips back into a wrinkled muzzle, exposing shocking pink gums studded with far too many yellow teeth. Those teeth snapped together, so close to my leg that they made an incision in the knee of my trousers as neat as any surgeon could have managed. I said a bad word, lashed out with the katsouna and jumped back ten feet – or that's what it felt like. Diogenes stayed hackling in the middle of the path for a minute or so. Then he slunk back into his oven and collapsed again with nose on paws, still grumbling, keeping both ears pricked and both eyes fixed on me.

I pulled up my torn trouser leg, but the yellow teeth had missed me by – quite literally – a whisker. I waited till the shock waves subsided, then inched forward once more. The head came up, the lips flickered, and the growling changed gear like a motorbike meeting the open road. I stepped back. Christ! What now? Then I remembered the slices of paximadia, dried rusk bread, in my pack, left over from today's picnic lunch. Cretan guard dogs don't exactly live off the fat of the land. I got a rusk out and threw it to Diogenes. It didn't bounce twice. Problem solved. I won't say he licked my hand as I passed, but there was no more of that lip business, and the drooping tail gave the ghost of a wag.

Argyroupolis, the City of Silver, is one of the most charming spots in Crete, a handsome little town among the mountains, perched on a hilltop above a valley shaded by big sweet chestnut and plane trees where springs of water come gushing and tumbling by the dozen out of ferny clefts in the rocks. The water is the liquid treasure of the City of Silver – it supplies the whole of the town of Rethymnon, and has spawned a clutch of tavernas around the sources, which have used the waterfalls for scenic effect with spillways, sluices and cascades. A steep zigzag path, lit by muted lamps by night, connects the upper town with its springs, and the whole effect is of one of those 'Little Switzerland' resorts at the height of some Victorian heyday. Yet you need only a glance around the town to see relics of a far more glorious Venetian past. Along the narrow streets one spots handsome doorways with beautifully carved capitals, fluted columns and elaborately bevelled pediments, some opening onto ancient vaulted interiors, others into wastelands of weeds. One carried the fading inscription 'Omnia Mundi Fumus Et V...' ('...mbra' was missing) – 'All this world is but smoke and mirrors'.

Nowadays it is Stelios 'Steve' Manousakas who makes things hum in Argyroupolis. Stelios is an archetype of a very particular kind of modern Cretan – a self-made man who lived away for years in Canada, making money in the restaurant business, and has come back to Argyroupolis with his French-Canadian wife Joanne and a nice wad of money to inject some pep and some prosperity into his home town. An ex-mayor of the place, a proprietor of tourist shops, restaurants and tavernas all over town, he can fix anything for anybody. Needless to say he, too, is a friend of Charis Kakoulakis. 'In Argyroupolis, Christopher, you will see Mr Manousakas and say that you are my friend. You will have no problems in Argyroupolis.'

Indeed the only problem I encountered in the bustling little town was finding a time when Stelios Manousakas could make himself available for a chat. 'Ten minutes, please, at my shop, OK?' In the event, of course, we sat in the archway outside his tourist shop for three hours, absorbed completely in our talk, while business went on all round us. The returned exile and successful entrepreneur could detail just what was needed for his little town – and by extension, for every town in Crete. Drive, imagination, an ability to see the bigger picture, a willingness to grasp those small opportunities for investment – classy little tourist shops selling soaps and perfumes made locally, decent rent rooms done out the traditional way but with proper mod cons, computers for the use of youngsters with a good idea. 'But many of us don't want to see that, or can't see that. It's kind of a problem all over the island; how do you get the brightest and the best to stay around and put their eggs into the Crete pot, rather than the Athens pot or the London pot? Or the Canada pot, come to that? And then they have to follow up the bright idea, make it really work. A lot of Crete isn't quite ready for that yet.'

The talk, as so often in Crete, turned to war – not the current NATO bombing of Yugoslavia, Stelios didn't want to open that subject, but the Second World War and how the Greeks felt about the British. Hitherto I'd heard nothing but expressions of brotherhood and mutual goodwill whenever the topic of the British and the war in Crete had been raised. Didn't you help us drive out the Germans? Weren't there many brave Englishmen fighting alongside our andartes? We are friends, you know! Good health to the British, and let's have another! Perhaps unwisely, I made reference to the old shepherd of the Nida plain and his pleasure at discovering, as he thought, that my father had been with the Cretan resistance. Stelios clearly had other ideas, and took pains to redraw the emotional map for me.

'The English are not necessarily regarded as heroes because of the war, you know. The Germans certainly did bad things – for example, they destroyed Kallikratis, where you are going tomorrow. But it must be said that their message when they came was: Leave us alone, and we'll leave you alone. Many men joined the resistance, left their house and family, went to the mountains. Many suffered, many died.' Stelios spread his hands, palm up. 'Then when the world war finished and the Greek civil war began, what happened? The English supported the Greek government, the King, all the forces of reaction. The Greeks saw some people who had collaborated with the Germans given positions of power, given influence and opportunities. ELAS, that was our pro-Communist party, it was defeated, and many good patriotic wartime andartes were killed or discredited. And the people saw the British supporting this. They remembered how at Yalta, Churchill had carved up the world with Stalin and Roosevelt, and Britain had taken Greece as part of its sphere of influence. Lots of Greeks didn't like that, and they didn't like the English very much.'

'But what about Crete?' I said. 'I've never heard a word of this anywhere I've been in the island.'

Stelios shrugged and stirred his coffee. 'Here in Crete it was different. It always is! We didn't want to fight each other – we had only isolated incidents, somebody shot here or there. There wasn't the same bitter struggle. So maybe feelings against the British were not so strong, and maybe that's still true today. All I am saying is – if you really want to know Crete and the Cretans, you must be realistic and hear all sides. Don't expect to be treated with special friendliness when you come to Greece, just because you are British and we fought on the same side in the war.' He looked up under his brows. 'This is real history I'm telling you, not some romantic bullshit. That's the way we felt, as Greeks.'

That evening, on kafenion TV in the town square, a reiteration by NATO of its five demands of Serbia – to stop the killing in Kosovo, to withdraw its forces, to accept a NATO-based international security force, to allow refugees to return, and to work towards a permanent political solution. The spokesman's harsh, intransigent, uncompromising American voice crackled out: 'Mr Milosevic has only one exit strategy – to say to our five demands: yes, yes, yes, yes and yes.'

Leaving Argyroupolis shortly after dawn the following morning, a little sobered and subdued, I passed a number of deflated but still sheep-shaped hides, complete with fleece, skin, hanging blue sinews and blood streaks, laid limply over the roadside fences to dry. The road west ran through the shady Grigaris gorge towards Asi Gonia, home village of George Psychoundakis, the 'Cretan Runner'. Psychoundakis's entire flock of sheep was stolen from him after the war, and he endured many vicissitudes, at one low point working as a navvy building the gorge road to raise the means of living for his family. It was during his work breaks, and during quiet periods at night in caves and shelters along this road, that his masterly account of his years in the resistance, *The Cretan Runner*, took shape. I looked around me, picturing the slight figure crouched scribbling by the flicker of an oil dip, as I walked on into the borders of Sfakia, that harshest, highest, least compromising and most macho of all the regions of Crete.

If the lowland country of eastern Crete is a ripe fig tree sheltering in a sunny garden, and the central upland a steadfast olive tree nurturing a rich harvest of fruit against the wind and weather, Sfakia in the south-west of the island is a grim and knotty old prinos in a dry crack of the mountains, tough, durable and prickly, carrying the threat of a sharp spike for any intruder. The aspect of Sfakia is rugged and hard, a bare south-facing coast cut with fearsome gorges that rises steeply out of the ink-blue Libyan Sea and climbs for 8,000 feet to a roof of pale, parched mountains. Nothing is easy. Fishing on the rocky coast is unpredictable, shepherding in the remote mountains fraught with hardship and danger. People have to grab what they can, when they can.

The story the Sfakiots tell about themselves neatly encapsulates their personal mythology. When God made the world, He dealt especially kindly with the people of Crete, for whom He had always a soft spot. Olives were His gift to the folk of Sitia and Selinos, the east and west ends of the island. To dwellers in the low northlands of Crete He offered grapes and wine, to those in Amari the succulent figs and cherries. And lo! He looked on His work and saw that it was good. 'Hey, Lord!' complain the Sfakiots, arriving before His throne all riled up and armed to the teeth as usual. 'What do *we* get, apart from these dry rocks You've dumped in our corner?' God smiles a half smile and beckons the Sfakiots close. 'Listen,' He says, 'don't you see, you fools? You just sit here among your rocks while the good people of Sitia and Selinos cultivate their olives, the northlanders their grapes and the men of Amari their fruit trees. Sit tight and silence your empty bellies until every other place in Crete has got its harvest in. Then,' says God, 'you Sfakiots can run down there and pinch the lot!'

Talking in the taverna on the beach at Kato Zakros, the night before I set off on my walk through Crete, I'd mentioned my intention of passing through Sfakia towards the end of the expedition. The taverna owner, a native of east Crete, had produced a wordless comment I'd sometimes seen before when Sfakia was under discussion: a bending and flexing of the right arm to mime formidable strength, accompanied by a screwing of the left forefinger into the side of the head to imply craziness. Mainstream Crete looks on Sfakia with a mixture of admiration, disapproval and a patronising kind of amusement. Sfakia returns the compliment, with interest. To Sfakiots, traditionally, the rest of Crete seems a pallid, limp-wristed kind of place. Sfakia is the only country for a proper man, and these men do their best to live up to the image. You'll see more beards, more black shirts and baggy breeches, more leather knee-boots and twisted sariki headbands in Sfakia than in all the rest of modern Crete put together. Historically Sfakia with its rugged mountains and remote fastnesses was the main centre of resistance to invaders. There is still strong local pride in stories of Sfakiot rebel leaders, from possibly mythical ones like Kandanoleon and his ghastly death by hanging at the cruel hands of the Venetians after being captured at a drunken wedding celebration, to Daskalogiannis and his ghastly death by flaying at the cruel hands of the Turks after he had upset the Pasha of Iraklion. Spend any time around the village of Koustogerako in the mountains above Sougia, and someone will tell you of how when the Germans had the women and children of the village lined up for execution in September 1943, Kosti Paterakis fired a miraculous shot from his hiding place nearly a quarter of a mile away which killed the machine-gunner and put the Germans to flight. Kosti's brother, eagle-nosed Manoli, one of the most famed and feared resistance fighters and a valued colleague of George Psychoundakis and Patrick Leigh Fermor, died in his hale and hearty old age long after the war, tumbling from a peak as he chased an aegagros. Even though Koustogerako lies over the border in the neighbouring province of Selinos, this was the ultimate exit for a Sfakiot hero. On kafenion walls and in private houses throughout Sfakia the likenesses of these palikares still hang in amateur etchings, flyblown daguerreotypes and fading black-and-white photographs. Their fierce spirit still pervades the region. The inter-family feuds that used to plague much of upland Crete have virtually disappeared from the island, but some still smoulder in the Sfakian mountains, usually sparked off by sheep-stealing or land encroachment. From time to time someone gets hurt, or is 'persuaded' to leave their village along with their family; every now and then someone is shot. Sfakia is not a place for milksops.

In Asi Gonia the old men sitting on their narrow kafenion chairs under the plane trees looked tremendously impressive with their sweeping moustaches and curly katsounas. The tarmac ended a few hundred yards beyond the village, and the dirt road commenced a steep seven-mile climb into the hills to the west. I climbed with it, sweating buckets, stopping every hour to get the pack off and take a slug of water. At every hairpin bend on the steep, shadeless road I tipped my hat to a new angle to keep the sun off my already stinging face. Unseasonably hot weather for May, the locals had said. I hoped it had melted the snow on the high desert of Lefka Ori as well as roasting me. The steep grey mountains I could see rising in front looked daunting enough, but I well knew they were really only foothills. Up at the pass, staring ahead, a familiar trick of perspective kicked in; the rugged grey mountains shrank as if sucked downwards into the lower country, while the pointed heads of the central mountains of Lefka Ori rose behind and above them, streaked and whorled with snow, like hooded bullies peering over the shoulders of the juniors to watch a playground scrap. They did look very snowy still. Tomorrow night, with luck, I would be sleeping near Askifou, the start of E4's climb into the central desert of the White Mountains. A phone call then to Pantelis would settle whether the high crossing would be feasible or not.

The mountain village of Kallikratis, one of the remotest in these hills, lay among its trees in a hidden valley. A summer village, inhabited from May till November by shepherds and the tenders of olive groves and vine-yards, its tiny population of 30-odd had just arrived for their six-month tenure. Everyone relied for transport on rattletrap pickups and a selection of donkeys and mules. Walking the dirt road through the village I saw large numbers of abandoned houses, tottering Turkish archways opening on to mildewed, roofless rooms, sun-cracked doors hanging drunkenly open. Under tangles of fig branches, heaps of stones from half-collapsed walls lay where they had fallen. What could have brought such ruin to the place?

Black-shirted and handsomely moustached Stelios Giannakakis, vigorous in his late middle age, received me at his kafenion with real hospitality. Pantatosakis? Of course I know the man! A true palikare – he has trodden every stone in Crete. Any friend of Pantatosakis is a friend of mine, end of story. You are hungry? Tsikoudia first – that's what we call raki in these parts. *Yia-sou, Christophere! Yia mas, Stelios!* Now: salad, bread, misithra, some chips, some wine. That's the best I can do for now, I'm sorry. Where are you staying tonight? Sleeping out in that little bag? Not at all! You'll sleep *to spiti*, at my house. Nonsense, not another word!

In the long, lazy afternoon I turned to the Psalmist on the kafenion verandah. He was inconsolable: in utter, abject misery. 'My days are consumed like smoke, and my bones are burned as a hearth ... By reason of the voice of my groaning my bones cleave to my skin. I am like a pelican of the wilderness: I am like an owl of the desert. I watch, and am as a sparrow alone upon the housetops ... For I have eaten ashes like bread, and mingled my drink with weeping.'

Stelios's sons and friends sat tight in the shade inside the kafenion, watching TV. The rumble of explosions and wail of ambulance sirens came faintly out to the veranda where Christos, the older brother of Stelios, sat beside me and drank coffee. I laid my little customised phrasebook on the table and cranked up a halting conversation, amplified with plenty of hand signals and facial contortions. Why were there so many ruined houses in Kallikratis? Was it just the result of depopulation, of the hardships of the shepherding life? No, said Christos – it was the Germans, back in 1944.

'I was about 8 or 9 years old then. Up in the hills around were the andartes, fighting the Germans however they could. There was one Englishman who stayed up there that we called "O Tom" (Tom Dunbabin, the senior British officer liaising with the resistance groups in Crete). He was very fierce with the Germans. I used to go up where he was hiding and bring him milk. The RAF planes would come over at night and drop everything the andartes needed – clothes, food, equipment, arms, radios.

'The andartes pulled off a big coup in the spring of 1944 when they captured the chief German, General Kreipe, and took him over the mountains to Rhodakino and then away to Egypt. It was a great triumph for them, but it brought trouble here later on. The Germans came to Kallikratis, thousands of them, in October, and they blew up and burned all the village. They shot some people, too, including women – about twenty men and about ten women, I think. I was only a boy, but I remember taking Stelios – he was 3 years old – and going up into the mountains to be safe. These houses that were blown up ... some have never been rebuilt, as you see. For us they have become a sort of memorial, I suppose.'

The TV explosions abruptly ceased as the set was switched off. A couple of old men came stumping onto the veranda, angrily expostulating to each other. I thought they were having an argument with each other, but then the words 'Kosovo' and 'bombas' emerged from the tirade. One of them caught sight of the fair-haired stranger. Yermanika? Amerika? Oh, English! Listen, I fought alongside the English during the war, but this is too much! Do you know what we have just seen in there? It's intolerable! NATO are fascists, no better than that. Where will it end? What do the Americans think they are doing? What – are the Balkans their colony? Come on, what do you have to say to me, eh?

What would have happened if I had been able to muster a cogent defence in decent Greek? Such was his fury, the grandfather would probably have struck me with his stick. My lack of a tongue saved me. Oh, terrible! War is bad – very bad! No war! My poor platitudes didn't please the old man, but neither did they bring his anger to the point of explosion. He glared at me with contempt. Humph! Is that all you can say? Huh! You're a disgrace to the Englishmen I knew. Pathetic! And with that he turned on his heel and marched off.

Later I learned the cause of his rage. A NATO airstrike had hit a civilian convoy in the early hours of that morning at Korisa, a village near Prizren in Kosovo, killing nearly ninety Albanian Kosovars. The film of the aftermath, originally broadcast on Serbian TV and replayed all over Greece, was the most graphic and disgusting yet shown. It struck me forcibly, and with shame, how quickly one could isolate oneself in these wild mountains from events in the wider world. Only last night I had sat in Argyroupolis and shivered to hear the stony American voice of the NATO spokesman dictating what Mr Milosevic's response to the organisation's demands must be: yes, yes, yes, yes and yes. Today I had not even thought of Kosovo. Absorbed in Christos Giannakakis's account of the war of sixty years ago, I had taken the TV explosions and sirens for the soundtrack of a Hollywood film.

I woke in the middle of the night in desperate need of a pee. I was hunched up under a blanket on a carved bench twenty feet long that ran the length of the Giannakakis house, a single large room spanned by a great Turkish arch of stone. Striped rugs covered the concrete floor. A wooden ladder stood propped against the sill of the elevated, open-ended compartment where Stelios slept. Other cubbyholes and cubicles had been formed with clapboard partitions, and in these lay half a dozen family members or maybe more. Before dropping off to sleep on my bench I had registered them vaguely as politely smiling shapes flitting past to their alcoves in various stages of night attire.

Problem: the lavatory was outside across the yard. How was I going to traverse and get out of a darkened house full of sleepers behind flimsy partitions, then do the whole thing in reverse, without waking the entire family? Obviously you can't, I told myself, so just turn over and go back to sleep. It never works like that, does it? The urge to empty my bladder, as is the way of such things, became more imperative the longer I lay and tried to conquer it. I slipped out from under the blanket and stole across the room. One of the rugs almost tripped me, but I recovered my balance at the expense of a stubbed toe. The front door was of a design that incorporated a sheet of opaque glass loosely inserted into a metal frame. It rattled like the devil when I put pressure on the door handle, but I got it open, slipped through and closed it again without mishap. So far, so good.

After seeking and finding the sweetest of relief, I re-entered the house and eased the front door silently shut once more – or would have done, if the night wind hadn't crept playfully up to seize it suddenly from my grasp and slam it shut with an almighty bang and rattle. Everyone stopped

When I sat down in Kallikratis

'The Germans came,' said Christos, miming
dynamite or flames, disaster
roaring upwards. On his middle finger
blood gleamed: a milking accident.

'The houses – pouf!' Beyond the terrace, stone
doorways gracefully arched
open arms of hospitality, though
their walls slumped into rubble.

'They shot the women …' Grumbling in black, an old
man heaving himself along,
goat on a rope, stooped for stones to fire
at dogs prying among the ruins.

'I hid my brother.' At the other table
Stelios yawned, stretched his legs,
nodded to me. Inside, his boys sat close,
watching a television war.

'Serbia – bad!' Crackle of flames, raw crash
of houses, widowers weeping, boys
clinging together: this was what I found
when I sat down in Kallikratis.

snoring, groaned, turned over, sighed, sat up. What the hell …? Father, is that you? What's going on? Oh, it's that vagabond, that Englishman. Well, really, I know they're all supposed to be mad, but this is a bit much. Do you know what the time is? It's all right for gentlemen of leisure like you, but the rest of us have to be up early – you know, *work*? Ever heard of it?

Most of this, of course, took place only in the theatre of my skull, behind my burning cheeks. In point of fact the Giannakakis family, far too polite to remonstrate with the stranger within the gates, sighed quietly once more and recomposed itself for sleep. Meanwhile, feeling like the bounder in an H.M. Bateman cartoon – 'The Man Who Raised Cain And Didn't Care' – I crept back to my bench, too abashed to remember the Greek for 'sorry'.

Next morning I bid Stelios goodbye. He wouldn't accept a penny for the two good meals and the night's accommodation, but modestly asked if I might send him a copy of the photograph I took of him. I cast around for E4, and found it very fulsomely signposted out of the village. Unfortunately, as I discovered a mile or so down the path, this was an alternative sidetrack leading down to the south coast. The main E4 route, west out of Kallikratis towards the White Mountains, ran innocent of all indications. For me the hopelessness of European Hiking Route E4 waymarking had long become a standing joke, a jolly jape. But I found that at this advanced stage of the journey, three-quarters of the way through Crete, I didn't really care. The dirt roads, kalderimi, dusty paths and village lanes had somehow turned out to form their own heterodox highway to the west, quite passable and even reliable if one simply gave oneself up to it in faith and hope.

Faith and hope were needed, too, on the many-headed road across the hills from Kallikratis. I tossed a coin at a couple of turnings and threw paximadia to a couple of wolfdogs that ran across my path, and arrived in the village of Askifou full of self-satisfaction and confidence. That lasted only as long as it took to get through to Pantelis Kampaxis on the crackly public phone. 'I am sorry, Christopher, but I have spoke to Pantatosakis and to George Aphordakos. They say it will be too difficult to go to Lefka Ori because of the snow. I am really sorry.'

So that was it, the unassailable verdict. The south coast and the gorges for me.

In the evening the main square of Askifou is a pleasant place to sit under the aspen trees, watching the orange light of sunset fade on the eastern mountains. Four little kafenia surround the square; the village men wander very slowly between them or sit in twos and threes, joining or ducking out of a more or less public conversation as they choose, joking with passing acquaintances, shouting a response to hoots from friends going past in pickups, hawking and spitting, patting children on the head as they scoot by, chewing over weighty matters and trivialities. This expansive rumble and trickle and occasional explosion of men's voices, counterpointed by the lighter notes of the women sitting and chatting as they shell beans and strip mountain herbs on their doorsteps in the street behind the main drag, backgrounded by the birds chirruping the sun down in the aspens and plane trees, is the keynote of a Cretan hill village at this particular time of day.

Copper-coloured beetles were hatching out all over Sfakia. The species seemed very inefficiently designed. Any slight puff of wind would blow them over on their backs, where they would remain helplessly thrashing, at the mercy of any passing predator, until first one and then another claw would chance on an anchoring point and they would be able to flick themselves right way up again. They seemed programmed to climb everything vertical – trees, table legs, lamp posts, fennel stems, and my trouser legs as I sat with a cold Amstel beer and an aluminium dish of pistachio nuts. Three had made it round and up the overhang of the table-top, and were crawling in a rather aimless fashion across the tin surface as if uncertain what to do now. In my state of blissful idleness, and seeing that I had not only two protagonists but also a control group (albeit of only one participant), plus the means (the kafenion owner's charming daughter had just set a complimentary thimble of tsikoudia in front of me), I decided to carry out a scientific experiment. Do copper-coloured beetles get drunk, and if so, on what?

I blobbed a large drop of Amstel and a slightly smaller drop of tsikoudia onto the table. The 'volunteers' approached. All shied away from the tsikoudia like Blue Ribbon spinsters in a distillery. Their reaction to the drop of beer, though, was significant. Beetle One – the largest – sank its face into the Amstel, drank at least half, crawled off with no visible signs of staggering, and then stopped dead as if suddenly hit by an 'Oh-Christ' moment. Beetle Two, the smallest, drank the rest of the beer, crawled after Beetle One and leaped on its back, initiating a bar-room brawl (or was it a priapic orgy?) that had them grappling all over the table in an inextricable embrace. Beetle Three, meanwhile, ignored both beer and brawl, made for a peanut and remained clamped to it, licking the salt.

Conclusion: beer and peanuts are better for you than hard liquor, but may still lead to trouble.

At my lodgings I found my eyesight no longer permitted me to pass the end of a thread through the eye of a needle. I tried for twenty minutes, then asked the taverna owner's wife if she would kindly do it for me. With Herman Munster stitches I contrived to sew up the rip that the Diogenes of the oil-barrel kennel had torn in the knee of my walking trousers, and went to bed determined not to mind too much about the snow and the White Mountains. It wasn't a very peaceful night, though. The Askifou nocturne consisted of the customary barking of the village dogs, the dinging and donging of sheep bells from a fold on the mountainside, and the sounds of *l'amour* through the wall of the neighbouring bedroom where an enviably inexhaustible French cyclist who had ridden all the way up from Iraklion that day (so he'd boasted) was doing his best to ride all night long, too. He made both mattress and mistress squeak till dawn.

Eventually I gave up the struggle to sleep, fetched the *Odyssey* from the backpack and had it finished by first light. Though the Psalms had proved my staple literary fare throughout this walk, Homer had given me a lot of fun, too, and a breath or two of inspiration. If any couple ever overcame a superabundance of trials and tribulations it was Odysseus and his Penelope, reunited at the winning post after being parted all that time. Our hero dealt with the weaselly suitors and with the sexually collaborative handmaidens of his house in terrifying style, too. And that wretched goatherd Melanthius who'd sided with the opposition. God, what a way to die. There was no doubt about it; whatever about Odysseus being born in Ithaca, the man was clearly a Sfakiot, and a black-shirted palikare to boot.

Blissed-out contentment from the Psalmist in the morning. The self-abasement in the dust, the eating of ashes and drinking of tears had been abandoned in favour of sublime praise of God's creation: 'God who layeth the beams of his chambers in the waters: who maketh the clouds his chariot: who walketh upon the wings of the wind ... he watereth the earth from his chambers. The earth is satisfied with the fruit of thy works! Wine that maketh glad the heart of man, and oil to make his face to shine. The trees of the Lord are full of sap; the cedars of Lebanon, which he hath planted; where the birds make their nests: as for the stork, the fir trees are her house.' The Psalmist even went so far as to smile upon the ocean, so often a terror to him. Today he was happy to eulogise 'this great and wide sea, wherein are things creeping innumerable, both small and great beasts. There go the ships,' rejoiced the Psalmist, 'there is that leviathan, whom thou hast made to play therein. These all wait upon thee ...'

It was the sea I was longing to set eyes on today – the Libyan Sea of the south coast, glimpsed from the summits of Thripti and Psiloritis and from many a pass and high viewpoint over these past five weeks, but never actually encountered. It was a short walk, but a spectacular one, down to the sea from the village of Imbros, winding into the bowels of the earth through the snaking contortions of the Imbros Gorge.

Before entering the gorge I bought a copy of the English translation of the local guide to the chasm, a publication intended to attract foreign tourists, but so Sfakiot in spirit that it featured among its illustrations a graphic shot of a couple of butchered sheep with the alluring caption 'Slaughtered Animals'. In fact, for the final and definitive summing up of the Sfakiot character, one can't do better than turn to this guidebook: 'Heroic people ... the purest in Crete. Tall, slim people with a look of intelligence always present to accompany their hard characteristics. They are egoists, ambitious, liberal and generous. They, rightfully so, have a high self esteem. When their pride is insulted they will not think twice. They will sacrifice everything they own, even their lives, a way of showing that they will observe and preserve ancient customs and traditions. They are well known for their hospitality, and their true love for big feasts and beauty.'

Once into the Imbros Gorge I dropped 2,000 feet in a couple of hours through the rock-walled canyon, so narrow that at one point I stretched out my arms and found I could touch both sides at once. Down this shadowed cleft in May 1941 passed thousands upon thousands of Allied soldiers, thirsty and exhausted beyond coherence after a three-day forced march from the north coast under repeated air attacks, hoping against hope to be evacuated that night or the next from the tiny south coast harbour of Chora Sfakion. A wartime tin helmet hung by its chin-strap from the branch of a tree as I passed, as if abandoned there only an hour ago by its owner.

Out over the sheet of flood pebbles at the bottom of the gorge, and on west to Chora Sfakion with the sea on my left hand. A big moment, this. From now on the Libyan Sea would always be there, an infallible guide over the last eighty miles or so. The map (and why did I imagine I could trust it now?) showed a confident, unmistakable red line, unbroken and unwavering, hugging the shore from Chora Sfakion all the way to journey's end at Hrissoskalitissas, the Monastery of the Golden Step. No ifs, no buts, no ins and outs. E4, you beauty, you're coming good at last!

The Gorges of the West
(Chora Sfakion to Paleochora)

*'The Lord answered me, and set me in a large place ... The Lord
hath chastened me sore: but he hath not given me over unto death.'*

Psalm 118

On holiday in Crete in the summer of 1973 my father found himself
standing one afternoon on the concrete ferry slip at Chora Sfakion,
with many things passing through his mind. During his service in the
Mediterranean as a destroyer officer in May 1941, his ship *Hero* had been
ordered to Alexandria for repairs after being badly near-missed just before
the evacuation of Crete. So Dad had not been present off Chora Sfakion
during the four frantic nights at the end of the month, when some 10,000
Allied soldiers were snatched by the Royal Navy from the beach in front
of the little capital village of Sfakia. He had, however, helped to evacuate many thousands of troops from tiny ports and lonely beaches in the
Peloponnese only a month before, after the fiasco of the Allied landings
in mainland Greece. Many of these survivors had taken straight across to
Crete to strengthen the garrison there before the German invasion began.
At the height of the Battle of Crete *Hero* brought new reinforcements
to the island on the night of 26 May, dodging her way into Suda Bay on
Crete's north-west coast among the burning wrecks and floating corpses.
One of the Army officers on board was Evelyn Waugh; and it was one

of Dad's private amusements that the commando intelligence officer who was sick in his canvas washbasin on the passage to Crete was the future author of the classic fictional account of the Cretan débâcle, *Officers and Gentlemen*.

Pondering this and other all-too-vivid wartime experiences in these waters, Dad became aware of the proximity of another man of about his age, upright and disciplined in bearing, evidently an Englishman, obviously ex-Services. This person, too, was staring around him as if old memories were being awakened.

'It looks as if you'd been here before,' remarked Dad.

'Yes,' returned the other man. '1941, May, Battle of Crete. I'll never forget it. And you?'

'I was around here, too,' Dad said, 'in the Navy.'

The man stiffened and glared. 'Bastards!' he said. 'Bastards! You left us behind!'

⤳

Standing in my turn on the Chora Sfakion ferry slip, I took a long glance across the tight cluster of white houses and tavernas to the brown slopes that rose dramatically at the back of the town. In caves, holes and hollows the shattered men from Britain, Australia, New Zealand and Greece had crouched by day in hiding from air attack, emerging each night to join the more or less patient lines waiting on the beach, each man straining to spot the arrival of the boats and landing craft that would ferry them out to the darkened ships. A few sour notes developed. There were a couple of unsuccessful attempts to sneak into the boats out of turn, to pull rank. Some stragglers faked wounds to gain priority. On the whole men behaved as they had proved to do throughout the war so far – doggedly, decently and with bitter humour. But some scars lasted, especially among those who could not be embarked before the Royal Navy's margin of safety ran out. My father never learned which unit his interlocutor had belonged to, but he was certainly one of the unlucky ones who had been left to fend for themselves. Some found shelter in mountain villages, at the risk of their hosts' lives; some made their way to welcoming monasteries such as Preveli, back along the coast to the east. Many were spirited away from Crete, one way and another. But, said Dad, he'd surmised that this man must have been one of the 12,000 or more who ended up enduring for the following four years the long-drawn-out misery of prisoner-of-war camp. What could my father say? He had murmured something conciliatory, and disengaged himself.

Dad, like so many of his generation, disliked talking about the war. But this pungent little scene, one he would allow himself to rehearse from time to time, had always stuck in my mind. Now, walking on through Chora Sfakion and fending off the blandishments of importunate taverna waiters ('Sir, you from Germany? From England? You want room, very cheap?'), I thought of Dad, and the millions of servicemen and women like him, who found when they emerged from the strange and intense adventure of the war that they had left an irretrievable piece of themselves behind.

On a bend of the road beyond Chora Sfakion an E4 sign stood up proudly on its black-and-yellow striped pole. A large-bore rifle bullet had punched a hole with gleaming edges of raw aluminium through the centre of the waymark square. The pellets of a shotgun blast had turned the remaining tatters of the sign into a fine-mesh sieve. 'Shepherd people like to shoot many signs in Sfakia,' Pantelis Kampaxis had warned me, and here was the proof. Sfakiots are notorious for gun-toting; if there is not quite a pistol in every pocket, there's certainly a gun in every sheepfold. However, no matter how riddled the sign, it was there, and I found it reassuring. Likewise the black and yellow stripes on the rocks ahead. I left the road, and plunged along a narrow ledge that swung in and out of clefts in the mountainside, now scraping my right elbow on the rocks, now with my left boot heel overhanging space. This was fantastically exhilarating. The coastal landscape had me gasping: tremendous rocky bluffs and gorges marching inland, orange and grey rocks the size of houses that had tumbled down from on high, headlands enclosing tiny bays of grey pebbles only to be spotted from this path or from a boat at sea. Way out on

Sweetwater

Yesterday he checked his cache, the old
Canadian. Climbed far above the shore
into the yellow synclined cliff, rolled
away the stone and found tent, stove,
lamp, the long spade bundled in a
place apart as he'd left them. Saw
no angels, though he might have in that high
niche over Sweetwater near the sky.

Tends the beach like a gardener, his mind
seeing more than pebbles. Looks for little; makes
something from nothing. What the devil brings
he'll deal with, living stripped, seeing if
the sun can clean him, knowing how to find
under the dry stones the sweet springs.

the southern horizon two islands floated in a dreamy grey mist – Ghavdos and its neighbour, Ghavdopoula. As for the path: what had seemed at first the roughest of haphazard sheep tracks gradually revealed itself, by its subtlety in always choosing the best line, as a cleverly engineered, carefully buttressed, well-surfaced kalderimi – the old coast road from Chora Sfakion, in fact, built when donkeys were the only driven things in Sfakia.

Down to a beautiful green sea as clear as glass, on a long curve of pebbles under huge yellow cliffs that stood crumpled and squeezed into vast folds of rock. 'Sweetwater, they call this place,' said Bob, the elderly curly-haired Canadian I fell in with. 'I'll show you why,' and he took my katsouna and dug it deep into the pebbles. Fresh water welled up in the hole, dark and shining. I tasted a palm-full, as sweet and cool as a mountain spring. 'Just arrived here for this year, so I've been landscaping,' Bob said, indicating the flat area of pebbles he'd smoothed off with his spade to make a foundation for his tent. We sat and chatted, basking in the heat of mid-afternoon. This was the sixth year Bob had come to spend the summer at Sweetwater. 'We live simple here,' he said, looking out over the hazy sea, 'and we live naked.' Sitting action to words, he let drop the towel he'd gathered round his waist as I came up. Looking round I could see other naked men, lone figures on the wide beach.

'I'm retired now,' Bob said. 'I'm spending my pension exactly how I want. I cache my gear each winter when I go back to Canada – a tent, the spade, some cooking things, you know – up in the cliff there, in a little cave, and I climb up and get it when I come back again in the spring. It's always there.'

'What do you do for things you want, food and so on?' I asked. 'Well,' allowed Bob, 'I do walk over to the town now and again. But I don't need much, and I don't *want* anything. I'm aiming to shed wanting stuff. All I need is the sun and to get clean, to live cleanly, do you know what I mean?'

First-class hippy gobbledegook, was my first thought as I crunched away across Sweetwater beach – just the sort of nonsense I haven't had to hear for the best part of two months. God, is this what the south coast is going to be like, a transatlantic New Age shitefest? But the barren hillsides, the empty shoreline and the milky blue sea rebuked me. I began to be ashamed of my cynical reaction, and to turn Bob's laconic words over in my mind.

Looking ahead I could see a tiny white toenail at the foot of a great sunlit cliff, a perfect single curve of buildings, roadless and silent, framed between bushes of papery purple rockrose. As a paradigm of peace and quiet, there was no beating this. A big shark-nosed ferry from Chora Sfakion was thrumming into the bay at the head of its wake, another crescent of shining white. I walked into Loutro just ahead of the disembarkees, got myself a room with a nice seaward balcony, dumped the pack and flaked out on two chairs with a groan of satisfaction. Three days to go to my 50th birthday, and I couldn't conceive of a better place to celebrate that curious event.

When they bring the road to Loutro – if they ever do; there has been talk of it for decades now – Crete will lose something extremely precious. You just can't mix tour buses and tranquillity. And there's no doubt that the little port, if one can even dignify it with that title, would be a major attraction for mass tourism, what with its pretty white hotels, its handful of seafood tavernas on the beach, its delicious semi-circle of a bay, and the giant hillsides of grey and orange that cradle it round and catch the warmth and light of the sun from dawn till dusk.

Loutro is a transhumance village of the modern age. The sheep (well-heeled, well-mannered English and Germans of the middle classes, the former distinguishable by their white pot sunhats, voluminous shorts and thick novels, the latter by their minuscule, religion-revealing swimming slips) are boated in from springtime onwards, and the locals give them their grazing, tend them and milk them of their money. Then when the weather turns nasty the sheep are boated out again and return to their winter quarters in Southwold or Landshut. The trouble is that there aren't nearly enough sheep in this little tourist flock to satisfy some of the locals. 'Increase the flock,' is the cry. 'The pasture can stand it. Bring 'em in by road and let's have another line of hotels squeezed in behind, or up on the cliff above there. Oh, it's a protected archaeological monument, the site of ancient Phoenix from which St Paul's ship was blown in the most famous gale in the Bible? Yes, OK, but who actually goes there? Where's your visitor numbers? Where's your *bottom line?*' Local politics being what they are in Crete, money will probably do the pleading and secure the judgement in the end. But for now only the bass drumming of the ferries and the occasional snarl of a fisherman's outboard engine disturb the deep pool of Loutro's peace.

I fossicked around in Loutro for the best part of five days, tending my battered feet, easing my pack-belaboured shoulders, yarning with my neighbours and letting the sun and sea breeze exorcise the quite appalling stink from my walking boots, now banished to the outermost corner of my balcony. I also did a little navel-gazing in quiet hours alone on the scrubby hillsides or kicking among the stones and pottery shards of Phoenix. Fifty seemed an age when a lot of men woke up to find they hated themselves and the life they had dug themselves into, an age of displacement activities, of big red motorbikes and small blonde 'friends'. What did I feel about it? Not a lot, was the answer I came up with. What had changed in the last ten years? I'd become greyer, wider, quieter; more amused at myself; more interested in what made people tick, good and bad. More aware than ever of the power of music and laughter to break down barriers. More opinionated, maybe, but – thanks to all those years spent exploring the backlands, the islands and odd corners of the world – even less inclined to paint myself into any one specific religious or political corner. Before setting off on this walk, I'd have certainly said that I'd become more cautious, but now I felt quite differently about it – the fear-strung ditherer of Kato Zakros seemed to have got something of a grip on himself at last, and for that I could thank Jane and her wonderful, unselfish present. Family things, as ever, turned out to be the source of the greatest pleasure and the sharpest pain. That seemed about the sum of it – no great revelations, after all. But something to ponder: a raking through of ballast at a halfway point in the voyage, perhaps.

On the evening of my birthday the neighbours treated me to dinner, and we had a bit of a party. A 'cake' made its appearance – an almond tart with one tiny candle in the middle. Our genial hotel-owner Vangelis poured us a brimming tsikoudia all round, and left the bottle on the table. Cue many songs and much hilarity, followed by a measure of skinny-dipping by moonlight. Ah well, you're only young once.

'Would you please fetch that stick of yours?' said one of the waiters. 'I've been wondering about it – where did you get it from? Oh, Kritsa, that's over in Lasithi, isn't it? Yes, this is a real good katsouna. My grandfather, he's a shepherd up in Lefka Ori, he'd appreciate this. You'd better look after it!' Another admirer of my plain white figwood katsouna! I turned it over in the lamplight, looking at its many scars and splinters. The rocks of the Cretan mountains had splayed its business end like a superannuated toothbrush. It was hard to imagine now how I would have fared without this faithful, silent and trustworthy companion, so often dropped, so often forgotten and gone back for.

Beautiful Katsouna

It was the way men praised you: 'Poli orea –
really beautiful!' – quite openly admiring
your white curves, your slenderness,

picturing themselves holding you.
'How did a man like you,' they asked me outright,
'get your hands on her?' It made me proud,

not jealous. 'Picked her up in Kritsa ...'
That was how it started. Now we have been
walking out together for many years;

have had our ups and downs. At my right hand
you've crossed the Cretan mountains, stamped the dust
of stony roads, pointed out the path;

steadied my hundred stumbles, never wearied
the way with chatter. On quiet moonlit floors
you've shared my sleeping mat. As for those dogs,

you boldly threatened them, or bravely met
the fangs that scared me stupid. There was one time
I left you; but I hurried back, knowing

how much I'd miss you. These long miles have changed you,
friend and companion – aged you, some might say.
Yes, you carry scars now, lines

that tell of the hard road we've come together.
Those who know what beauty is, salute you.
Katsouna, they call you: beautiful Katsouna.

Now for the final hurdle – the series of great south coast gorges that cut across the westward thrust of E4. According to the map I could just skirt the coast, crossing the gorge mouths one after another, nice and simple, easy as pie, job done. But now, remembering the solemn warnings I'd had from Kitsa and Pantelis about the section between Agia Roumeli and Sougia, and looking more closely at the concertina folds of contours coiling in brown loops down from the mountains to the coastline, and the purplish blush of shading the cartographer had added around the gorge clefts, I could see it wasn't going to be quite such a stroll in the park as all that. How could I tackle it? Those gorges looked scary but splendid, and I thought I could see a way to wriggle up one and down the next so as to cut out the bad bit of the coast with a great high loop into the White Mountains and back. 'Faragi Samarias', the upward gorge was labelled, 'Faragi Agia Irinis' the return one. I'd walked the Samaria Gorge years before, and vividly remembered it – Europe's deepest and most impressive gorge, 6,000 feet of fall, with thousand-foot walls which approached each other at their narrowest point so closely that with fully extended arms you could almost touch them simultaneously. 'Doing the Gorge' had become Crete's Number One tourist adventure. Back then I'd done it the conventional way from top to bottom, inching down on somebody's heels with someone else's breath on my neck, one component in a long, long snake of walkers. This time it would be an upward climb, fully laden. A bit of a slog, but no particular problem, I thought. The Agia Irini gorge I'd never even heard of, but it looked long and deep enough. Better get in a little practice first – and here at hand, just to the west of Loutro, was Aradena, the exact gorge for the job.

A beautiful south coast dawn of pink and pearl found me high above Loutro, climbing the zigzag kalderimi that stitched a zip scar up the face of the 2,000-ft mountain slope. It was wonderfully cold on the hillside, still blanketed in its night shadow. The village shrank away below until a curve of the mountain shut it out of sight. The sea lay flat under an oily sheen, the influence of the still unseen sun running its hues from inky black to grey, from dazzling silver to the ice blue of a gannet's eye. By the time I had topped the ridge and was looking down on the mountain village and plain of Anopolis, the sun was up and firing the hills into gold.

In the village square stood a statue of Daskalogiannis, 'John the Teacher', a little round cap on his head, a pistol and a dagger thrust jauntily into his cummerbund. The Sfakiot hero who led a revolution based on Anopolis against the Turks in 1770, he died under the flaying knife after upsetting the Pasha of Iraklion with an impassioned rant about the woes of Crete and its Christian sons and daughters. I sat at a taverna table with a cup of coffee and a bowl of yoghurt, regarding the noble profile of Daskalogiannis outlined against the slopes of the White Mountains. High and far above, the inner peaks stood against the blue sky, now streaked more with the pale grey of limestone than the white of snow. The hot spring sunshine of the past few days had evidently been doing its work, but all too late for me. I gazed on the summits, sighing, wondering if I would ever set eyes on that high desert heartland that I had so long feared and looked forward to.

~

Seven years were to pass before the hollow eyes of Daskalogiannis once more stared through me in the village square at Anopolis. It was October 2006, and I was in the passenger seat of a juddering 4×4 being driven by expatriate Frenchman Jean Bienvenue. We were headed into the mountains, bumping up the dirt roads of Lefka Ori to the very top of the highest shepherd's track. There we'd leave the pickup and strike out on foot, climbing higher into the heart of the massif. It had been niggling away at me, this hole I'd left unfilled since the spring of 1999, and here was the chance to put the last piece of the E4 jigsaw in place.

Up through the upper limits of the prinos, up to where the greenery died away and the naked limestone began to contort itself as if volcanic convulsions had torn it apart. The pale cones of Kakovoli and Trocharis, of Mavri Laki and Sternes reared high overhead, all of much the same shape and slope. Rough screes stubbled their flanks. Between them and around on all sides rose and fell the extraordinary landscape of the high desert. Sinkholes lay everywhere, some opening lips like those into which I had tossed stones on Psiloritis, others dropping away to form black, glassy-sided potholes of enormous depth. Dark grey pinnacles and humps of rock lay between the sinkholes. To be wandering these badlands in fog or snow would be inviting disaster. I could see very plainly now why even mountaineers as experienced and fearless as George Aphordakos and Iannis Pantatosakis would hesitate to venture here in spring, with patches of sun-rotten snow concealing as many sinkholes as they revealed.

The beauty of these harsh highlands was breathtaking, and so was their isolation, more than 7,000 feet above the sea. We followed the red blob waymarks of a shepherd's track due north below the pale heights of Pachnes, summit of the Lefka Ori range, a mountain that tops out at 8,048 feet – just ten feet lower than mighty Psiloritis. The locals, naturally, are having none of that, said Jean; it is practically a duty for every true Sfakiot to carry a stone with him when he climbs Pachnes, in order that the summit cairn shall one day look down on that insignificant little anthill away in the soft and spineless east.

Three figures appeared ahead on the track, dark blobs in the pale landscape – a shepherd carrying a long-barrelled rifle, his big bristling sheepdog, and a black mule slung with panniers full of this summer's cheeses. The shepherd passed us with a gruff 'Kalimera, good morning,' and a sharp glance out of the corners of his eyes. These solitary men still live the hard mountain life, seeing few others than fellow-shepherds in the high desert, pasturing their flocks and boiling milk in the mitato to make superb graviera cheese. One sees them squatting on the rocks with a gun across their knees, or at a great distance striding the vast mountainsides with their weapon held across the shoulders and behind the neck in the crooks of both elbows, their dark figures indicated by the bright scarlet dots of their sakoulis or woven wool haversacks. The path that Jean and I were following is one of their main routes to and from Anopolis. Nowadays scarcely distinguishable to the untrained eye from the dusty land through which it runs, it was the chief trade route between the Sfakian coast and the north-west of Crete until all-weather motor roads made it redundant. Snow falls thickly and lies long up here, and the heartlands of Lefka Ori are only really viable for pasturing between May and October, even in these days of 4×4s and heavy-duty tyres. Those can only get you so far up the mountains; after that, as for all the bygone generations, it's mule-back or Shanks's Pony.

In the heart of the hills the trail dipped down through a gorge to reach Katsiveli, a cluster of mitata at a crossing of tracks. The cheese huts were round and stone-built, their doors now locked against the oncoming winter. On the ridge above stood a small mountain refuge, also locked. 'You have to bring the key with you from the EOS, the Alpine Club in Chania, if you want to use the refuge,' commented Jean, 'but usually the people who need this hut most are the ones who haven't planned a stay – walkers who get caught out by a storm or by nightfall. Especially when they're trying to follow E4, naturally!'

Beside the mitata the north-south track meets the one that I had hoped to follow with George and Iannis seven years before, the 22-mile E4 route through Lefka Ori from Askifou in the east to Omalos at the head of the Samaria Gorge in the west. Here stood a familiar object – an E4 waymark pole, its tin plate sign shot to ribbons. 'Shepherds,' shrugged Jean, 'they're not into pleasure hiking, and they don't like strangers.'

A glance at the maps showed the problems of following E4 through these barren and all but deserted regions. The dodgy old 1:100,000 that I'd used during my long walk simply ran its familiar scarlet line blandly across the mountains. Only the scrawly legend 'Achtung! Weg ohne Markierung! (Warning – unmarked path)' hinted that something might be tricky here. The second map I'd brought today, a 1:25,000 sheet by Anavasi, was a lot more realistic, with notes on sources of water in summer and advice on how to negotiate or sidetrack the most tiring, obscure or downright dangerous parts of the route. The high desert of Lefka Ori is a place of unearthly beauty, but far and away the wildest part of Crete – in fact, although it is only just over twenty miles from east to west, it's one of the wildest places in all Europe. On a clear day like today, in the company of a guide so experienced in these mountains that even the local shepherds ask him to bring them news of their sheep, the traverse of the high desert looked formidable but feasible. On one's own, in snow or fog, it would be tantamount to begging for trouble.

∽

Sitting in the square at Anopolis on that hot spring morning in 1999, I found it hard to tear my eyes away from the simple majesty of the White Mountain peaks. Eventually I got up and followed the road out of the village through the olive groves where a young shepherd, busby-bearded and saturnine, stood chin on crook contemplating his flock in a timeless pose. He looked every inch the same stock as the fierce andartes one sees in old Second World War snapshots, or those etchings of such leaders as Daskalogiannis that hang half obscured by dusty glass behind kafenion counters.

The road led west to Aradena, an abandoned village on the lip of the gorge I was aiming to follow back down to the sea. A splendidly maintained kalderimi brought me down to the gorge floor in a series of sharp hairpins, and once down there between rock walls hundreds of feet high there was only one choice of path. Goat corpses and fallen prinos trees littered the bed of the chasm, and almost at once an appalling crash of noise rumbled overhead as if Poseidon the Shaker had decided to pull the whole thing down and start again. I ducked, instinctively, and waited for the boulders to come tumbling. But it was only the sound of a car passing over the wooden slatted decking of the bridge that spanned the gorge.

From here on it was pretty much plain sailing, until the sides of the gorge closed together and became impassably choked with a huge boulder fall. There seemed no way through. But red splodges of paint indicated a pathway down across the boulders, a slip-and-slide progress that ended at the rim of a hundred-foot drop. I peered over. A flimsy iron ladder forty feet high ran down the face of the fall, and another halfway down continued to the bottom. Not exactly a Health and Safety exemplar, but it was all there was. Do it now, or go back the way you came. Hanging the katsouna on the ladder a few rungs down, and gripping the plastic bag containing

Two Cretes

Man in a yellow teeshirt, right of shot,
lounging on two chairs under the gridded

shade of the café awning; to the left,
murmurous with beer on this hot

afternoon, two lovers touching knees;
backdrop of mountains, hard and dry as rusks;

centre-frame the blue, the depthlessly blue,
the greener than blue Libyan Sea. I framed

this dreamy photograph, calling it 'Crete'.
Then thought of dusty roads, of sweating men

stringing their vines, cheeses in a cave
high in the hills, madness at those feasts

of wine and lyra, a shot in the night, sad skin
of a flayed lamb, raki in a priest's

glass, snores of a stranger, hands of a healer,
fear on a lonely track … and did not take it

water bottle and map in my teeth, I lowered myself over the edge and proceeded downwards, face to the ladder. Memo to self: bring a bloody backpack next time you do a day walk, you fool. I managed the first ladder all right, but halfway down the second one my hands, greasy with sweat and suncream, slipped off their respective rungs. Both feet slipped, too. A nasty moment. I found myself, ludicrously and improbably, reaching with outstretched lips for the rung in front of my face as it shot upwards and I fell downwards. Plastic bag, map and water bottle tumbled from between my teeth to the ground below.

Have you seen a three-toed sloth clinging to a cecropia tree? That was the embrace I bestowed on the ladder when I reconnected miraculously with it a few feet further down. The impact gave my arm sockets a wrench, but other than that all was well. Once I'd got to the bottom it took a few minutes to stop trembling. After a drink of water and a quick damage inspection I felt fine, and negotiated several more boulder sides (none as scary) lower down the gorge with a fair pretence at nonchalance.

Down at the beach I found a taverna and sat quaking. Still a bit shook up, are we? Yes. All right – before the coast walk back to Loutro, I prescribe a cold beer, a kebab and a bit of a sit. Thank you, doctor. Just tell me straight – will I ever play the fool again?

Off from Loutro at first light next morning, on the last leg of the journey. I found it strangely hard to get going again. The route of the coast path held no difficulties, but the path itself proved something else again, by far the worst surface I had encountered in Crete, a horrible rubbly mass of awkwardly shaped stones that skidded and stood on end underfoot. When I got to Agia Roumeli I sat down on a beach rock and had a good look at my boots. The scale of mutilation was astonishing. The rubberised seal round the toes had entirely worn away, making them leak like Liza's bucket. The stout leather uppers had been cut, scored and cracked into crazy paving by 250 miles of Cretan limestone. As for the soles, the constant jarring, abrading and digging in of hard dry stones had smoothed their hi-tech corrugations all but flat. They'd serve me as far as the end of the road, with luck, but after that they'd be fit only for the knacker's yard.

To Agia Roumeli my father had come in *Hero* on the night of 22 May 1941 to assist fellow destroyer *Decoy* in retrieving George II, King of the Hellenes, and his small entourage, after their desperate and difficult journey by mule over the still snowy upper regions of the White

Mountains. The capture of the King would have been a splendid coup for the Germans if they could have caught up with him, but in the event the royal party arrived safely on the beach and was taken out by small boat to *Decoy* and a night passage to Alexandria. Dad didn't get to embark the King of the Hellenes in his own ship, but he never forgot the drama of the approach in the darkened *Hero* to the mountainous coast looming in the night, the tension of waiting offshore, and the relief as the two destroyers turned and made steam for the Egyptian coast with their precious cargo. The Psalmist's daily commentary, as I read it on the ferry slipway at Agia Roumeli almost sixty years later, had never seemed more apt: 'Our soul is escaped as a bird out of the snare of the fowlers: the snare is broken, and we are escaped.'

In Agia Roumeli I couldn't find a room for love nor money. This small, roadless village at the foot of the Samaria Gorge is entirely concerned with catering by day for the tens of thousands of walkers who pour out of the gorge each afternoon from April, when the flood waters have subsided far enough to make things safe in the canyon, until October when the Samaria Gorge National Park authorities generally take the decision to close the gorge to walkers until the following spring. By nightfall almost everyone has caught the ferry to Chora Sfakion and their bus back to Chania, so that there's little incentive to provide accommodation. This proved a blessing in disguise, since I was obliged to catch the ferry to the next place down the coast, Sougia, and from the deck was able to get a really close and lingering look at what I'd ducked by choosing the gorge route over the coast 'path'. The coast of Selinos did look absolutely daunting, wildly rugged, slashed with two cruel gorges and many smaller ravines, rock stacks and pinnacles, and countless mountains great and small that hid modestly away until the ferry, turning some lonely cape or promontory, opened up a view to reveal them in all their pale grey and green splendour. Where E4 lay among these savage scenes I could not guess, and neither, I felt sure, could anyone venturing in this coastal wilderness.

A quiet night in Sougia and a ferry first thing in the morning back to

Agia Roumeli, plying the same route in reverse, gawping anew at gorges and mountains lit by the eastern sun to reveal beauties and terrors that had been concealed by dusk and the westering sun the previous evening. I set off at mid-morning up the flood valley of the Samaria Gorge. It was an eerie sensation to have the most celebrated, the most crowded gorge in Europe all to myself. Things were so quiet that when the ticket man's dog took exception to me at the lower kiosk and demanded a pound of flesh with menaces, it was almost a relief to employ my pet phrase at pigeon-wakening volume: 'Pare ta skiliaaaaa!'

I came to the tremendous cleft of the Sideroportes, the Iron Gates, and stretched out my arms to their fullest extent as I walked through. You just can't help yourself, even though you can see clearly that you're not quite going to be able to touch both walls at once. Beyond lay the luck stone, covered as usual with tiny pebbles. I added one and walked around the boulder three times in prescribed fashion, making my wish as I did so. Around here, halfway to the abandoned gorge-bottom village of Samaria, I met the first of the walkers coming down. From now on it was hello and how are you, guten tag mein herr and bonjour madame, ciao bella and kalimera, excuse me sir and would you mind awfully, thank you very much, no, after you, every few seconds till I was nearly at screaming point. What can you do? Duck your face and play the miserable bastard? Then I hit on the solution: don't climb on like a prat with a thistle up his whistle. Lie down under that fig tree by this little run of water, put your hat over your face and catch forty winks. Eighty if you like. What on earth is your big rush?

When I woke towards mid-afternoon, the Samaria Gorge had reverted to eerie silence. Climbing it became a pleasure again, at least until I reached the foot of the *xiloskala*. The name means 'wooden stairway' but the old steps of wood have long been replaced by a good if very steep zigzag path. For downward walkers the xiloskala means a sharp and slippery 2,000-ft descent on skiddy stones into the upper regions of the gorge. For those coming up with a 40 lb pack on their back and flat boot soles, it's simply one sod of a climb. Near the top I heard the bubble and splash of the

Neroutsiko water

Slogging hangdoggedly up the gorge where
I had struggled since the climb steepened
on rubbly stones, sick with the sweat and effort,
I found you, Neroutsiko water,

gushing in a grooved stone basin
like something offered. I pushed my whole head
into your jet, made a channel of
my lower lip: drank and drank.

Traveller of deep pathways,
I looked up at last from your cold
complexity of taste – earth, rock,
ice, and something faint and sweeter –

and saw your parent snow, high in a shadebound
gully, ungenerous until the sun
called for you. Neroutsiko water,
you have wounded me, a Pyrrhic

dart. In all the cafés of the world,
by all the springs I'll mope, ceaselessly
drinking, endlessly unsatisfied:
never again to taste perfection.

Neroutsiko fountain, sank my hot face into its blessedly cold waters and drank as if I'd never stop.

After the 3,000-ft ascent from the sea with its nasty steep sting in the tail, the three miles of flat walking across the high plain into the village of Omalos seemed a doddle. Found room. Ate goat stew. Put head on pillow. Slept like tree.

In the morning the wind had veered round into the west and a cold grey morning lay spread over the White Mountains. It took me an hour to figure out a passage across the plain of Omalos, another of those flat saucers of upland grazing ringed by mountains and dotted with sheep and goat folds and little settlements of brightly painted beehives. Shortly after leaving my lodgings I met a most magnificent billy goat. His deep-toned neck bell sent out a hollow clanging as he flounced away, feathery shins all a-flutter like the chaps of a gay cowboy.

E4 signs directed me down a side track, a well-found kalderimi that brought me onto a hillside where all trace of the path had been wiped away by a giant and very recent landslide. Pebbles were still dislodging themselves and rolling down the fresh scree. The slip must just have taken place. What now? It didn't look stable enough for a mouse to venture across, let alone a laden walker. I took off the pack and sat myself down in Micawberish style. And sure enough, after ten minutes or so a couple turned up on the far side of the landslip. We gesticulated our intentions. I think you were first, Sir! No, you first! No, really, we can wait! No, I'm actually waiting for … for a friend, so do please have the first crossing! Gingerly they came inching across. Neither rolled screaming to destruction. I waited till they were well past me and out of sight before scampering across myself.

Somewhere hereabouts I passed from the province of Sfakia into that of neighbouring Selinos, a region less famed for bloody deeds and heroic resistance than Sfakia, but one capable of producing a clan as altogether redoubtable as the Paterakis family of Koustogerako, a mile or so away across the mountains. Whatever the region, the terrain remained hard to read and hard to negotiate. Waymarks led on to what I assumed was the upper entrance of the Agia Irini gorge. That was confirmed as the gradient steepened and fell away over rock slides and under fallen trees towards the unmistakable high walls of a Cretan gorge. At some point in the long downward scramble, I realised later, I must have passed the Chyrotrypa cave, scene of one of those tremendous tales of heroism by the palikares of the past, when brave local boys Pentaris and Marangakis held off a punitive raid by the Turks in 1822 for long enough to allow the women and children to escape. One of the heroes was killed after a lucky Turkish shot had damaged his gun; the other was smothered to death in the cave when the attackers, unable to winkle him out, lit a smoky fire at the cave entrance and choked him where he lay.

Pine trees provided all the foreground smell today. Other keynotes were visual – shocking pink bushes of oleander, papery leaves of maple and fig against the blue sky, sulphur-coloured butterflies in the clearings. Faded icons and many small coins lay on the church-shaped rock of Agios Giannis, a rallying place for local people living under punitive regimes since time out of mind. Widely spaced rest areas were provided with water taps; I tried one, and received a mouthful of metallic liquid hotter than any shower I had yet enjoyed on this adventure. The black rubber hose that supplied the tap had been lying baking in the sun, who knows how long for? The path leaped up and back down again, now high in the gorge wall, now down among the oleanders in the bed of the canyon. At one point I passed a tumble of car-sized boulders fallen from the walls, and marvelled at the thought of the flood that must have swept them all together at this point. The scale, the weight and the seemingly precarious balance of these huge masses of rock combined to make me feel extremely small.

At the foot of the Agia Irini gorge a road scooped me up and carried me unresisting all the way down to the tiny seaside resort of Sougia, a cluster of houses and rent rooms on a big beach of floury grey sand. I found a bed at Number One, Paradise. At evening, a bottle of cold Mythos beer in my hand, I stood out on the beach and turned my face to the White Mountains, now bulking against the eastern sky. Their ranges and slopes stood bathed in beautiful magenta light, cut abruptly with indigo slashes of gorges and the high black blobs of cave mouths. Up until today I had been among mountains the whole adventure long, for the best part of two months and almost 300 miles. From now on it would be a coastal setting till the end of the walk. As when I had faced the White Mountains from the peak of Psiloritis, I found my hat was in my hand in a bareheaded salute. These great ranges of Crete seemed somehow to demand it.

'Oh man,' slurred the boy on the beach below my taverna table early next morning, 'this is just too much, man.' Great shades of Leary! Was this the 1960s all over again? It could seem so, down in laid-back, go-with-the-flow Sougia. The boy and his friend sat on the sand in their dew-pearled sleeping robes, loose bags of cloth enclosing their dreadlocks. The one with the big Taliban-style beard sat cross-legged and straight-backed, meditating perhaps, or maybe just lost in the pinks and greens of sunrise. His chum continued to mutter, 'Too much – oh man, too much,' as he prepared their breakfast, the fattest and longest 'Camberwell carrot' I have ever clapped eyes on. If he had entered it for the Preposterous Spliff medal at the Hippy Olympics, gold would have been guaranteed. Long after I had finished my eggs and coffee and started to chat to Roger and Randi, its stink of smouldering pinecones continued to pollute the crisp morning air.

Roger was an interesting man. Dressed in loose silk shirt and fluttering eastern slave pants, barefooted, broad and fair-haired, he looked every inch the louche Irishman of a certain age, abroad upon his adventurous occasions. 'A couple of times a year my lady in Dublin says to me, go on, get out of my hair, I can see what's going on. Bring me something nice back from Crete, but I really don't want to know about anything else you get up to, OK? And I say, Well, all right, if that's what *you* really want ...'

As soon as he arrived in Sougia, Roger had hooked up with Randi, a Belgian woman perhaps 20 years younger than him, with a nice square face and gummy smile under a pert urchin cut. They'd shared a week of uncomplicated, uncommitted sex, and would part with no regrets when he moved on elsewhere tomorrow. The success of this sort of very casual liaison seemed to depend on keeping things light, amusing and flirtatious – little glances and secret smiles. No declarations, no follow-through – God forbid. Randi would take on someone new as soon as Roger's bangled wrist had ceased to wave goodbye from the departing ferry. So would Roger, as soon as he had landed at the next little beach resort along the coast. That was quite clear, and obviously part of the contract.

Looking around the beach and seafront of Sougia I could see twenty couples in various stages of entwinement. Were they all parties to such agreeable conspiracies? Out along the beach a colony of nudists was set-tling like pink seals among towels for a day's sun-worshipping. 'We call that the Bay of Pigs,' Roger murmured, following my glance. 'All those pink bodies lying out snoring all day, shagging in the caves – you know.'

I felt like writing to *The Times*. What the hell was going on? How dare he, and she, and they, and those boys with their reeking Camberwell carrot? How could they do this to beautiful Crete? It took a little walk and a little me-to-me talk to get back my sense of perspective. You've been too long away from the coast, too long in the mountains with your head in the clouds, that's all. Too long among Cretans. This isn't Katharo or Thronos or Kallikratis, you fool. Don't be a prig. Of course this is how people go on when they're on holiday by the sea. Just be thankful it's all still small-scale, gentle and good-humoured. When they build a casino here and a motorway to bring the punters to it – that'll be the time to get the 'Yours, Disgusted' letter-paper out. What are you – a middle-aged man, all of a sudden?

That night I ate good fish with Roger and Randi, and we yarned long and tall over the pink metal jugs of wine. It turned out a great night, and I was sorry to say goodbye to them the following morning. But something was still bugging me as I started out on the long day's march from Sougia to Paleochora. I nailed it finally as I sat in ancient Lissos, thinking things over, in the ruins of the temple of Asklepios, god of healing. Somehow the mountains and their people, the green upcountry plains, the rushing cold air, the hard work and courtesy of rural men and women, the indig-nant lectures, a bloody fleece, a bowl of beans, a bed on a bench under a Turkish arch – mountain Crete, harsh and difficult as I had often found it, had got to me, got under my skin and into my bloodstream, as the cosy coasts would never do. The sea was beautiful, the little coast towns pic-turesque, the sand warm and the living easy – for visitors, at all events.

Dream rooms

'Dream Rooms' – someone thought that up, knowing
just what south coast drifters want:
nothing too real.
Slip in and out of the
little white towns, in and out of beds barred
with afternoon sun in dream rooms;
play in dreadlock caves, tamarisk camps,
lazy bays of pigs pink and tufted
under the sun's lens.
Soft dreamers' land, after
the rocky absolutes of mountains and their people.

But the mountains had soul. When I got to Paleochora, a charming old town straggling along a promontory around the golden stone walls of a Venetian fortezza, the first bed for the night I could find was in a house whose neon sign proclaimed, with many a curlicue: 'Dream Rooms'. After 'Number One, Paradise', that seemed to hit the nail exactly on the head.

Late that night, a paradigm shift. Out from the self-absorption and self-righteousness of seven weeks in my own company, and into the jolly social stew of a football crowd. I fell in with a bunch of friendly holiday-makers from Cologne, and we went off together to watch the European Cup final on kafenion TV. Not one ragged Kosovar corpse or wretched bereft Serbian mother tonight – in fact, since reaching the coast I had heard neither hide nor hair of NATO, nor of Slobodan Milosevic, nor of Beelzebub Beel the big bad bugaboo. Those ardent confrontations, those bitter harangues and passionately held opinions, seemed part of the life I had left behind in the mountains.

I was amazed to see it was Manchester United – Jane's team – against

Bayern Munich. I hadn't even realised that United had their hats in the ring. It was brilliantly exciting. Bayern led 1–0 from the sixth minute on, and played a very subtle, very tight defensive game. It looked as if it wasn't going to be United's night. Then they scored in the very last minute. Then, unbelievably, again in injury time. Wild scenes on the screen – the goalie doing backflips, one of the goalscorers dancing with the cup on his head, the granite-faced manager grinning from ear to ear. Best pleased of all were the German lads alongside me. They whooped, they cheered, they threw back their beer and yelled for more. How could this be? 'Because,' roared red-faced Günter, 'we are from Westphalia, and we like to see those Bavarian snobs to get smashed! United! United!'

At some o'clock past midnight I walked up alone to the fortezza and stood looking back at the mountains. A fantastic yellow moon floated there. I found oleander petals in my shirt pocket and tears on my face. Strange days.

Of Earth and Dreams
(Paleochora to Hrissoskalitissas)

'Praise the Lord from the earth, ye fire and hail; snow, and vapour; stormy wind fulfilling his word; mountains and all hills; fruitful trees and all cedars; both young men, and maidens; old men and children; praise ye the Lord.'

Psalm 148

On with the boots on a late May morning, on along the road for the last step of the way. The great mountains were behind me now. Bare cliffs of orange rock and long grey ridges guarded my right flank as I followed the sea road west; a scrubby coast of tamarisk, bamboo and dwarf pine, among which unfinished buildings bristled with roof rods and ranks of tattered plastic greenhouses grew cucumbers and tomatoes. Builders' yards; a go-kart track closed for the winter that looked as if it might never open again; a few downbeat rent rooms. A subfusc coast that hadn't managed to drag itself into the reviving sunlight of tourism. Its shabbiness didn't bother me. Somewhere not too far ahead, a dozen miles perhaps, lay Hrissoskalitissas, the Monastery of the Golden Step, my journey's end. One foot in front of the other and I'd see it, between one swing of the katsouna and the next.

Suddenly I was tired – bloody tired. A half-finished rent rooms offered itself in a dusty chicken yard. I got a room and sat poleaxed on its grubby

The tattered map

The map is fraying now, its creases
fluffing apart with daily sweat soak.
Sfakia is soon to be an island; Ghavdos
will fall off the edge of the world.

It never was a good map; hopeless liar,
rotten spiv of a guide. I know its
little indiscretions, its false economies of scale:
the hidden churches, invisible villages,
snake roads shown straight, uncharted plunge of
canyons into contourless shadow.

I can forgive the bad advice,
the lost paths that bruised my temper.
Now I read each line on its shifty face
more avidly than any traveller's tale.
These innocent whorls rise into the naked
peaks that made my breath catch;
this green streak chasms into a gorge
packed with boulders where I crept,
overawed, a morsel in a giant throat that
might clear itself with one tremendous choke.

I have hated that map with a whole heart,
have sworn at it, have roared with rage,
bamboozled, forced faute de mieux to be its
silly dupe, mile after mile.

Three more days, and I can be quit of its
dumb insolence. Then I will fold each
tattered fragment as carefully as bridal lace,
carry it home, and treasure it like gold.

little balcony all day. But I couldn't sleep. When I did doze off, it was to dream of Hrissoskalitissas and its golden stairway. By six in the morning I was gone. Last day on the road, with the cracked boots flapping and the map breaking apart at the seams. I scarcely needed it now. E4, having played the haughty paramour for so long, had come over all cuddly and close on this final day. Striped poles abounded, tin signs glinted in the sun, rocks and trees carried brave stripes of black and yellow as if it was Cup Final morning.

Summer had come to the coast of Crete. The grasses by the path were dry and weightless, the fields brown, the air full of dust devils. Shepherds parked their pickups on the rocky fields among congregations of madly bleating sheep and unloaded green stuff they had fetched from the mountain plains. The pale grey flanks of the hills quivered in heat haze. I followed the stony path down past Crio, where I had been told that springs of fresh water surface in the bay. As if on cue, a fisherman out in a long green boat dipped a plastic container in the sea and raised it dripping to his mouth. Drops flashed from his arms like diamonds. It seemed a kind of miracle.

Stumbling across thick sand, scrambling over rocks and pushing through tangles of juniper, I came to Elafonissi, the Island of Deer. 'Oh, ruined! Completely ruined since they allowed the cars to drive down,' grumbled a Frenchwoman who was sharing the shade of an olive tree with me. 'Now when I first came here, thirty years ago ...'

Elafonissi is one of those places that people cherish in jealous recollection. Over a taverna table in Paleochora one of the jolly Germans had confided, with misty eyes: 'Elafonissi, now ... that's a place with magic, plenty of magic.' So it had seemed to adventurous visitors in the 1960s, when they found the track around the hillside and followed it down to find the scimitar-shaped isthmus flanked by white beaches and a limpid turquoise sea. A lonely place, a few lucky people's secret. Now a dirt road had been pushed to the water's edge, and half-built hotels were beginning to march seaward. It was a time of lamentation among those middle-aged children of the golden past. But for me this day, shirt off and wading into that beautiful sea, all was bright and touched with enchantment.

On now along the road, through the dusty coastal plain, out to the westernmost corner of Crete. A block of white, a holy citadel raised high on a rock – Hrissoskalitissas, floating like a ship on a silvery sea of olive leaves. Churches, houses, monastic cells, storerooms all huddled together, a dazzle of white under a cluster of bright blue domes. I sat down on a rock, staring. The map, what there was left of it, showed the thin red line of E4 running on northwards for another thirty miles or more before burying its head in the Gulf of Kissamou between the peninsular horns of the island of Minos. And then where? Over to Cyprus, back to Greece, out into the wild blue yonder? I didn't know. My false-hearted lover had put me through the mill all right. I had tasted magic because of her, all the same, and was thankful. Now she was out of my system. Go where she would, I wasn't following.

I climbed the long stairway that I had dreamed of, gilded from top to bottom in brilliant sunshine. Whatever the state of my heart and soul, it seemed an irrelevance now to look for the golden step. In the monastery courtyard the solitary monk of Hrissoskalitissas came hurrying to greet the stranger. Dressed in a dusty and much-patched blue cassock, his mage's hair and beard floating in a soft white cloud behind him, there was a saintly and at the same time an earthy air to Papa Nektarios – Father Sweetness. Welcome, my friend! You look a little tired. Here are raki, sweet biscuits, water, apples. Where have you travelled from? Hah, that's a long way. Where will you sleep tonight? Why not here? Certainly there's room – one old monk can't sleep in twenty cells, you know!

The cell was spartan – a lumpy bed, a wooden door nailed and shuttered, a small hatch for communication with the outside world. To me it seemed perfection, a simple end to a long and ravelled journey. Dog-tired and drained of steam, still I couldn't sleep that night. Somewhere inside, the spring of energy still bubbled. I sat on the monastery wall, looking across the valley to where black outlines of mountains rose into a starry sky, until the mightiest of yawns almost broke my jaw in two.

Bells woke me, clashing the day to life. Up on the windy terrace Father Sweetness was laughing out loud and hauling bell ropes as if bracing round a set of celestial topsails. It was Pentecost Sunday. In a little while I would haul my wind and square away for other shores. But there was something to do first, a seal to set on things. In the monastery church, in front of a thousand-year-old icon of the Virgin, a cornucopia of offerings lay heaped on a lace mat. Among taximata and lucky charms, between a marriage ring and a tiny golden heart, I placed the sea-smoothed pebble I had carried across the island of earth and dreams.

Author's Note

The bombing of Yugoslavia by NATO in 1999 lasted from 24 March until mid-June, a couple of weeks after I had returned home from Crete. By then NATO was considering a ground invasion, although US President Bill Clinton was reluctant to commit American troops. However, Finnish and Russian negotiators finally persuaded Yugoslav President Slobodan Milosevic of the seriousness of the threat of invasion, and he agreed to allow a military presence, KFOR (Kosovo Force), into Kosovo. This force, under UN auspices but containing NATO elements, incorporated troops from France, Germany, Britain, Italy, the United States and Greece.

On 12 June 1999 KFOR began to enter Kosovo. Within three weeks some 500,000 refugees, mostly Albanian Kosovars, had returned home. By the end of November all but a handful were back where they had fled from in the spring, finding when they returned that most of the Serbian Kosovars who had been their neighbours – up to 250,000 people – had in their turn fled over the Serbian border for fear of reprisals.

Accurate casualty figures are hard to come by, but best estimates are that NATO strikes killed over a thousand civilians during the campaign. They also caused up to 5,000 military casualties. NATO casualties amounted to two US helicopter pilots.

Mass graves of Albanian Kosovars killed by Serbian forces were found in Serbia as well as in Kosovo. Estimates are that up to 10,000 may have been killed.

President Milosevic was deposed in 2000, and went on trial in The Hague the following year, accused of genocide and crimes against humanity. He died on 11 March 2006, before his trial could be completed.

Since 1999 Kosovo has continued to be administered by the United Nations. At the time of writing (spring 2007) its future status – whether as an independent state or as a part of Serbia – is still being debated.

As for the Cretan section of European Hiking Path E4 – it is far more widely mentioned online nowadays than was the case in 1999. A few more walkers have ventured its baffling byways. But reports suggest it is fundamentally no better waymarked, no easier to follow than when I set out to see where it would lead me. No reliable guidebook in English yet exists – that potential best-seller is waiting to be written by some intrepid soul. E4 could be the Pennine Way of Crete, or the Coast-to-Coast – a much-loved, much-travelled path. At present it remains elusive, enigmatic and fluid; a challenge to all comers, infrequently attempted, seldom accomplished. With all the imperfections and inherent difficulties of the path, there is no more entrancing way to discover the Mediterranean's largest and most magical island. However, E4 offers no guarantees of safety or success. So perhaps it is just as well that it remains in an unfinished and unpolished state – a rare diamond in the rough.

Acknowledgements

During my long walk through Crete I enjoyed so much hospitality among Europe's most hospitable people that I'd need to write another book to thank them all by name. I would especially like to thank these kind friends and acquaintances:

Aglaia Hill of Bristol for helping me to learn some Greek.

Iannis Pantatosakis and Kitsa of the Iraklion branch of the Greek Alpine Club for helpful advice on the vagaries of European Hiking Path E4.

Very special thanks to Pantelis Kampaxis for his invaluable companionship in the mountains.

I am very grateful, as always, to Charis Kakoulakis for the long arm of his help, and to Maria, Dimitris and George for their hospitality.

Stelios Jackson, one of the few to have ventured the E4 path through Crete, distributes news on it and on all things Cretan through his admirable websites http://www.hellenicbookservice.com/Kriti/Kriti.htm and http://sjwalks.interkriti.org/

For help and Easter hospitality in Ano Zakros my thanks are due to Mr and Mrs Daskalakis of Hotel Zakros; in Ziros to the Kharkiolaki family; to Dimitri and Katerina of the Taverna o Pitopoulis in Prina; in Kritsa to Manolis and Argyro Tzanakis, Iannis Siganos, Stergios who gave me my white fig-wood katsouna, and to the mighty Aphordakos clan – especially George, Manolis and Rula. I'm likewise grateful to Archimandrite Stephanos Marankakis of Moni Angarathou; Manolis and Maria Piperakis of

Ano Asites; Stelios Manousakas of Argyroupolis; Stelios Giannakakis and his family at Kallikratis; Giannis, Manolis and Georgios Fasoulakis of the Lefka Ori Hotel in Chora Sfakion; Vangelis and family of the Blue House Hotel and Alison Androulakakis of the Hotel Porto Loutro, both in Loutro.

Jean Bienvenue gave me a memorable walk in Lefka Ori, and Papa Nektarios made sure I had somewhere to lay my head at journey's end.

Last, but by no means least of my friends in Crete, I'd like to thank Lambros and Maria Papoutsakis of the Taverna Aravanes in Thronos at the head of the Amari Valley, a fountain of good food, wine, music and delight.

And finally my love and thanks to my wife Jane and my family, who urged me to set out on this walk and encouraged me every step of the way.

I am grateful to Sheil Land Associates for permission to reproduce a passage from George Psychoundakis's inspirational book 'The Cretan Runner' (Penguin).

The poems 'Argyro peeling oranges', 'The olive fires', 'The high man', 'The hollow stone', 'Shepherd', 'Beautiful Katsouna', 'Two Cretes', 'Neroutsiko water' and 'The tattered map' were first published in Christopher Somerville's collection *Extraordinary Flight* (Rockingham Press, 2000).

ABOUT THE AUTHOR

Christopher Somerville is a writer, journalist and presenter. During the past twenty-five years, he has been threading Europe's most characteristic countryside paths, recording his experience in over thirty books – including two charming collections of poems. Somerville was Walking Correspondent of *The Daily Telegraph* for fifteen years and is the author of *Britain and Ireland's Best Wild Places*, *Somerville's 100 Best Walks* and *Greenwood Dark* .